Two Great ' and a Sha

The Unexpurgated Golf Letters of Mortimer Merriweather

Inspired and Collated

by

Clive Agran

Copyright © 2021 Clive Agran

ISBN: 9798545983988

All rights reserved, including the right to reproduce this book, or portions thereof in any form. No part of this text may be reproduced, transmitted, downloaded, decompiled, reverse engineered, or stored, in any form or introduced into any information storage and retrieval system, in any form or by any means, whether electronic or mechanical without the express written permission of the author.

Foreword

Mortimer is busy ironing his plus fours at the moment and has therefore asked me to pen this foreword. As you can tell from the number of pages that you will shortly have to plough through, the old boy has fired off a fair-few letters of late and his gnarled old fingers will therefore benefit from a break.

Before I go any further, there are a few things I should perhaps explain to you about Mortimer. Reading his letters, you might form the impression that here is a grumpy old geezer with too much time on his hands and nothing better to do than vent his frustration at his increasing inability to reach a fairway or escape from a bunker by annoying those in authority with his daft ideas and ridiculous suggestions. Well, you would be absolutely right because that succinctly sums him up.

As his age and handicap inexorably rise, Mortimer is undoubtedly becoming somewhat disenchanted with the world. However, although some of his letters display what appears to be intolerance, please don't be offended. A combination of gout and the yips has undoubtedly warped his mind but the upside of that is he has developed an entirely original perspective that has endowed him with a unique outlook. He's very much a man of his time unequipped to cope with political correctness, woke awareness or anything originating much after 1957.

But I don't want to sound too negative as, when you eventually get around to reading his letters, you may well be impressed with his originality and forthrightness. He thinks of things that would almost certainly never occur to any right-minded person.

Now might be a good time to explain why there aren't any replies to be found in the following pages. Well, with one or two honourable exceptions, they were just too dull.

Mortimer concentrates on golf because that has been the main focus of his life ever since his great grandfather Egbert left him a mashie-niblick in his will. Golf, together with Madeira wine and the occasional port, is what he lives for. Not content with having won two monthly medals and one mid-week seniors' Stableford in his four-score years, he has sought to bolster his legacy with the letters contained in this book.

Whether the name Merriweather rightfully belongs alongside Old Tom Morris, Ben Hogan, Jack Nicklaus and Tiger Woods in the pantheon of golfing greats is for you to decide. It might sound a preposterous notion now but just wait until you've read this book before you decide whether Mortimer Merriweather is a genius or buffoon.

Clive Agran

Contents

Page

Section 1 **Somewhat Offensive**   1

British Trust for Ornithology	2
Colin Montgomerie	5
Disney	6
Sunningdale	8
Mohammed Al Fayed	9
Dustin Johnson	10
Scottish Tourist Board	11
Sir Bruce Forsyth	12
Jimmy Tarbuck	13
Lloyds of London	15
Professional Golfers Association of America	17
St George's Hill	18
Prostatitis Sufferers' Association	19

Section 2 **Hugely Controversial**   21

Penguin Books	22
HRH The Duke of York	23
Nigel Farrage	24
Head of Bombing	25
Kim Jong-Un	27
Royal St George's	28
Jeremy Corbyn	29
League Against Cruel Sports	30
Pope Francis	32

Section 3 **Simply Preposterous**   34

Ewen Murray	35
St Andrew's	36
TaylorMade	38
Hassan Rouhani	40
Dr Ping	41

GCSE Examination	43
Calloway	44
Boris Johnson	46
Communist Party of Great Britain	48
International Olympic Committee	50
R&A	51
William Hill – Accumulator	52

Section 4 **Utterly Ridiculous** 54

Acushnet	55
Wentworth	56
British Museum	58
American Golf	59
Armitage Shanks	61
Golf Museum	62
Sotherbys	63
Royal Troon	65
Tee Manufacturer	66
Lewis Hamilton	67
PGA	68

Section 5 **Pure Fantasy** 70

Augusta National	71
Chubby Chandler	72
Open Championship Committee	72
Ronald McDonald	73
Desert Island Discs	74
Talent Agency	76
Bryson deChambeau	77
Antonio Guterres	79
Rolex	80
The Archers	81

Section 6 **Completely Daft** 83

Pfizer	84
Eton College	85
European Tour	86
Guinness	88
Sky Sports	89
FootJoy	91
Andy Murray	93
Ryanair	94
DJ Spooney	95
Blue Line Office Furniture	97

Section One

Somewhat Offensive

Dear British Trust for Ornithology,

I desperately need your help in persuading the golf authorities around the world to adopt new nomenclature for describing how many shots have been taken over par. In case you're not familiar with the Royal and Ancient game, I should explain that par is what a good player on a good day should score on any particular hole. For a short hole it's three, for a medium length hole it's four and for a very long hole it's five.

Exceptionally good players can, of course, score lower than par. One below par is a birdie, two below par is an eagle and three below par is an albatross. Because you know pretty well everything there is to know about birds, you will note the avian nature of the terminology.

Good, bad and average players frequently take a lot more shots than they should on a hole ... one, two, three, four, five or more. Bogey is not a particularly nice word but it's the one used to describe a score of one over par. Thereafter, the game betrays a paucity of originality by describing two over par as a double bogey, three over par as a triple bogey, etc., etc.

There is clearly scope for a more imaginative nomenclature here and continuing with the avian theme is clearly both desirable and easily achieved. Having given it a great deal of thought, I have come to the conclusion that one-over-par, which is presently a bogey, should instead be called a 'partridge'. I like it for two principal reasons: 1) It's just a bit more than par. In fact, it's a 'tridge' more than par. And 2) It will enable players who score a four on a short hole to say, "I had a partridge on the par three", which I think will cause much merriment.

What should also provide a lot of laughs is 'Great Tit', which I think is an apt name for what is currently called a double bogey. Thereafter, I'm hoping for suggestions from

you. In case you can't think of any, I've drawn up a provisional list of what I think would work well:
Three over par – presently triple bogey – a 'Shag'.
Four over par – presently quadruple bogey – a 'Ruddy Duck'
Five over par – presently quintuple bogey – a 'Fluffy-backed Tit Babbler"
Although with golfers anything is possible and former British Open champion David Duval recorded a nine-over par 14 on a par five in The Open at Royal Portrush a couple of years ago, I think we should probably stop at the "Fluffy-backed Tit Babbler", don't you? At least golfers will be able to say things like, "I had a couple of Great Tits on the front and finished with a Shag up the last."

Dear Deposed President Donald Trump,

Having had a bike nicked from outside my flat in West Hampstead 20 years ago, I can understand how you must feel about having an election stolen from you. The worst thing about it all is that it undermines your faith in humanity and you probably don't feel you can trust people anymore. It must be especially hard for you coming as it does after so many of your aides, assistants and advisors, not to mention that dodgy lawyer of yours, all jumped ship. You gave them respectable jobs in the White House and a chance to move on from their previous involvement in fraud, tax evasion, money-laundering and general criminality and they 'thank you' by dumping you in it. No wonder you get on so well with that nice Mr Putin, who also has good reason to be somewhat paranoiac.

Anyway, my advice is to abandon any idea of running again, forget the whole presidential thing and move on to something for which you have a real passion ... golf. I think you'll find that, relieved of the responsibility of leading the western world, your short game will benefit and the time saved by not having to attend boring cabinet meetings and tedious summit conferences will allow you to work on your swing. In the fullness of time you might well look back at the humiliation of not being granted a second term as a blessing.

Because you're in the hotel and hospitality industry, you will also be able to claim any green fees, trolley hire and range balls against tax. Oops, I was forgetting you don't pay tax. Never mind, not claiming any tax relief on these items can only enhance your image and silence those miserable critics within the golf industry – almost certainly high handicappers - who claim you're a megalomaniac just because you acquired Turnberry, Doonbeg and Doral and re-christened them Trump Turnberry, Trump Doonbeg and Trump National Doral.

Finally, there is an under-exploited course on the east coast of Scotland that is simply crying out for a massive makeover. Not only that but it also regularly hosts the British Open and is so embedded in the rota that even those snotty suits at the R&A won't be able to deny you the thrill of hosting the greatest golf tournament in the world. How does, "The Open at St Trumps" sound to you?

****

Dear Monty,

I've long been a huge fan of yours and would love to see you cap a magnificent career by capturing at least one major title. After all, Phil Mickelson, who can't be much younger than you, just snaffled another one. What's more, I think I can help.

There's nothing I can usefully contribute on the playing front as, frankly, I struggle off a handicap of 19. But my mother taught me a valuable lesson early on in life, which I've always found useful and would like to pass on to you now. She used to say: "Mortimer, no matter what happens, smile and be grateful you're alive." And you know what, it truly helps.

Like most other folk I've been through a lot in my life. What with never having passed the driving test, redundancy and piles, but I've always smiled and considered myself a lucky man. Frankly, with everything you have - a great talent, pots of money and a beautiful family - you ought not to be so grumpy, especially as you probably never have to pay a green fee or rake a bunker.

Okay, you're allowed the odd scowl when you miss a short putt, but the rest of the time you should try to appreciate the glorious scenery and be happy that you're playing golf. Millions of others can't, because their wives won't let them. When was the last time Mrs M. said: "Colin, you're not off playing golf again! You played Thursday, Friday and yesterday and now you want to play on Sunday as well."?
To golf as often as you do, travel all over the world, stay in the finest hotels, have all your equipment supplied free and be able to watch the best players close up, makes me very jealous. Whenever you feel fed up, just remember Agnes Merriweather and her splendid philosophy on life.

****

Dear Mr Disney,

Below is the synopsis of a feel-good movie I think you should make. It has the working title 'Caught Cheating'. I don't want millions for it, just a modest $100,000 and a decent part in the film.
The action takes place in Surrey, England in 2019.
To the outsider, Charles Salisbury's life seems perfect. Married to the lovely and very much younger Linda, he has two delightful children, a secure job with a bank and is considered a pillar of the local community. His crowning moment comes at a dinner at his golf club held to celebrate his appointment as captain. However, his world starts to fall apart when, minutes before he is due to make his acceptance speech, he is caught literally with his pants down in the locker room with Geoffrey, the new assistant greenkeeper.
He's thrown out of the marital home by his humiliated wife, sacked by the bank, expelled from his club and, worse still, he finds his favourite Ping putter (product placement

opportunity) broken and stuffed in a dustbin. Although almost broken himself, this last act of wanton vandalism motivates him to fight back.

With what little money he has, he buys a caravan and camps on a strip of wasteland adjoining the local municipal golf course. Unlike the toffs at his old club, the less stuffy working-class members of the municipal club welcome him.

Driven by a burning desire to revenge his humiliation and with little else to do, he practices golf for hours every day and improves bit by bit. He captains the team at his new club in their annual match against his old club and, fired by all that has happened, his inspirational leadership helps his team to their first ever success in the fixture.

Charles, however, doesn't stop there. Despite being over 40, his handicap tumbles to scratch but, because of what happened that night, he's never picked to play for his county. Then, against the odds, he comes through both a pre-qualifier and qualifier to earn a spot in the British Open. Despite a double-bogey six at the first hole, he has rounds of 69 and 67 to comfortably make the cut. After each round he returns to his caravan, which he tows behind his beaten-up old car. Alone, he stares at photos of his ex-wife, son and daughter, and sobs.

Another 67 in the third round puts him in contention and he tees off on the last day in the final pairing, still symbolically eschewing a caddy and pulling a trolley. As he holes a 20-foot putt on the 18th to clinch The Open, he sees his wife, son and daughter cheering in the stands as he lifts the claret jug as the end credits roll.

I think Brad Pitt would make an excellent Charles Salisbury and Keira Knightley would be ideal as his wife. I'm not fussed about which part I'm given so long as I get to play a bit of golf.

Dear Sunningdale,

It is on a matter of the utmost delicacy that I write to you and I would seriously be most grateful if you would kindly respect the privacy of all its parts.

My uncle, Sheik Rashid Binami Al-Binami, is presently living in Dubai but he is hoping to be living in the UK quite shortly if only for the most pleasing summer months. A suitable estate with top-notch facilities has been found for him in very lovely Surrey. He will be most happy there especially as he will be close to the famous Sandown Park where he will enjoy watching the horses.

Horses are his number one pleasure. Golf is his number two pleasure and so I ask what he must do to join your Great Club. He plays very frequently in Dubai and tells me he is averagely good at the golf game. He is most proficient from bunkers perhaps because there is much sand where he can practice.

My English friends tell me that there are often dress rules in such a famous club as the Great Sunningdale. My uncle is comfortable in western suits but his wives only wear traditional costume. Would they be allowed in or would they be obliged to wait in the car park while he is being friendly after doing his holes? Which brings me on to the question of family membership. My uncle has five wives and 12 children. Presumably they would be covered by one family membership.

May Allah allow your putting greens to flourish and bear fruit.

Dear Mohammed Al Fayed,

I know you're a huge fan of football, but I have no idea if you play golf. It's an expensive game but great fun. With your excellent contacts you should have no difficulty in getting into a club. Some are a bit sniffy about foreigners, but I seem to recall that you've applied for a British passport, which should speed things up a bit. Anyway, my purpose in writing to you now is to alert you to a great business opportunity connected with golf. Those who love the game are suckers for anything to do with it, particularly the famous courses where punters will pay ludicrous sums for monogrammed sweaters and even golf balls. Why should the golf clubs nick all this valuable business?

What I'm suggesting we do is make available to the public through your world-famous Harrods store, a range of products that are both unusual and yet have historic associations. For example, an egg timer filled with sand from one of the world's most famous bunkers, such as the one guarding the 17th green at St Andrews. By the way, that's a course in Scotland, not Birmingham's home ground.

Then there could be bottles of perfume based on water extracted from such famous hazards as the Swilken Burn, also St Andrews, and Rae's Creek at Augusta National in the USA. Aftershave, too, could be distilled from mowings shaven from the fairways of Carnoustie in Scotland and Pebble Beach in the States. The possibilities are endless.

The real genius is that these products only need contain <u>some</u> sand, water or whatever from these famous places. One grain per million or one drop per 1000 gallons would be sufficient to enable us to rightly claim that they contain the genuine article. Each packet would include a certificate of authenticity, signed by a respected individual widely acknowledged as someone of proven stature, honesty and integrity... you? Harrods, frequented as it is by wealthy toffs, would be an ideal outlet for our gear and I can see the egg timers being knocked out for something like £29.99, the aftershave for £69.99 and the perfume for £99.99.

****

Dear Dustin Johnson,

May I first of all congratulate you on your excellent golf. From tee to green you are undoubtedly one of the top players around at the moment. And, if you continue to practice conscientiously, I see no reason why you shouldn't improve and put yourself up there alongside some of the all-time greats like Jack Nicholson.

However, watching you on Sky television playing in a recent tournament in the US, I couldn't help but notice that you were tending to bend your right arm as you near the top of your backswing. In this respect, you've got the same problem as my mate Reg, who plays off 21.

Both you and he tend to spray the ball a bit when you do this. Frankly he does it more than you do but, there again, you take the game a lot more seriously than he does.

It helps Reg to imagine he's got a broom handle stuffed down the right sleeve of his shirt. You might care to try this and see if it makes a difference.

Lastly, I understand that you're finally about to get married to Paulina Gretzky. Congratulations. However, don't make the mistake I did and not tell your intended about your fondness for golf. I suggest you sit down quietly one evening, explain that you play a lot of golf and that this means you will be away quite a bit. In this way, you'll prepare her a bit better than I did my wife and avoid the ridiculous arguments every time you go off to play.

Dear Scottish Tourist Board,

I'm thinking of taking my wife and two children to Scotland this year for a holiday. We've never been there before and, although I gather it can be very cold, even in summer, I would like to give it a try if for no other reason than to find out what the kilted people really think of Nicola Sturgeon. By the way, I don't hear anything of Alex Salmond these days. Whatever happened to him? Probably gone to live somewhere warm, sunny and tax-free like that other Scottish patriot, Sean Connery.

Back to business. I took up golf about 10 years ago and, due to a combination of natural talent and sheer determination, have steadily reduced my handicap to the 19.4 it is today.

Anyway, I'm considering taking my half-set of Petron Impalas with me to Scotland but don't want to use up precious space in my little Fiat if there aren't any decent courses up there. Do you know if there are?

I appreciate it's unfair to compare countries, but we went to Croatia last year and found a couple of real beauties right next to the Adriatic. Are there any in Scotland next to the sea?

A couple of other things. Do you know if the rules are the same in Scotland as they are in England? I would hate to embarrass myself by accusing some poor jock of cheating if he's only doing something that's allowed north of the border. For example, I expect you're given more time to find the ball up there.

Finally, I understand Scotland has its own currency and bank notes. Would I do better changing my money in England or is the exchange rate no different in Scotland?

Dear Executors of the late Sir Bruce Forsyth,

As a very keen golfer, Brucie must have encountered the problem of trying to lift a ball off a bare lie with the attendant risk of sculling the ball. Not anymore. Thanks to the new club I've developed, bare lies will no longer cause concern.

With an almost razor sharp leading edge, made from cobalt-coated tungsten, this club is set to transform the scores of average handicap golfers and will enable even the humblest hacker to have and I quote, "a good game... good game". Geddit?

Why, you might wonder, am I writing to you? Well, designing and manufacturing the club was comparatively easy as compared with thinking up a name for it. To be honest I needed one that suggested that the problem of a lack of natural growth - whether grass on the course or hair on the head - was one that could easily be overcome.

Brucie demonstrated that a lack of natural hair need not be an obstacle in life, but something that can easily be dealt with; in his case, with a discreet hairpiece. In the same way, a lack of grass under the ball can be overcome when you use "The Brucie Scalper." I like the word scalper because it not only implies surgical-like precision (scalpel) but links in almost seamlessly, if that's the word, with "scalp", which in turn connects with hair.

The informal research I've conducted at my golf club suggests that the name is still a popular one that will help sell the product. Although "Brucie" is not a registered trademark, and because his image will not appear on either the packaging or the advertising (unless you'd like it to), I understand that I'm not strictly required to seek your permission to use it. However, as a courtesy, I thought I should at least alert you to the existence of the product and

enquire as to whether you would like to be involved in its marketing or promotion.
If nothing else, it will help sustain his memory for thousands of years to come and permanently link his name to the game he loved.

****

Dear Jimmy Tarbuck,

To be honest, I've never thought you were particularly funny, but my mother liked you a lot and thought you funnier than your compatriot, Billy Connelly.
Anyway, whether you're funny or not is irrelevant. What matters is you're a well-known name and that you play golf because I've developed a really exciting club that I know will interest you.
Called the 'Tarby Tosser', it's a speciality club specifically designed to cope with those awkward little flop shots over bunkers and the like where getting the ball to rise quickly is the priority and not much distance is required.
The 'secret' is the 78 degrees of loft, which enables the player to strike the ball really hard without fear of flying it through the green. The only serious problem we've encountered in the research and development stage is that sometimes the ball flies almost vertically off the face of the club and has on occasions struck the player both on the way up and, less frequently, on the way down.
To overcome this and obviate the risk of someone getting badly hurt and suing us, we've had to incorporate a shield. Originally this was made of the same steel/titanium alloy as the clubface, but we soon discovered that, being opaque, it prevented the player from seeing the ball both at address

and impact. We therefore switched to Perspex, which works fine except that occasionally the ball strikes the screen, which is good insofar as it protects the player but bad in that the ball bounces straight back down either onto the ground or, worse still from a scoring point of view, back onto the clubface, which technically constitutes a double hit and incurs a penalty stroke.

My real purpose in writing to you is to enquire as to whether you would wish to become involved in this project as an investor and promoter.

Dear Mr Merriweather...
Your jokes are funnier than mine... Piss off! Yours
Jimmy

Dear Lloyds of London,

I presume most, if not all, of your members are golfers. Even the women! That's a good thing because golfers more than any other category of human being understand the tricky business of risk/reward. For example, there's a pond guarding the green on a par four and to carry the pond and reach the green is a distance of, say, 148 yards. Do you take out a wood and go for it or lay up with something safe like a five iron? That's the sort of tricky risk/reward calculation we golfers have to make somewhere in the region of 18 times a round.

And golfers understand the nature of insurance better than, say, tennis players because, 1) an errant golf shot can do a lot more damage than a mistimed volley, and 2) tennis players can't score a hole-in-one and are therefore never required to buy a round of drinks for a large bunch of thirsty strangers.

The other factor that I know will enhance the appeal of the proposal I'm about to make is that golf club membership is ridiculously expensive and, if you join an absurdly posh club with top-notch facilities such as fresh towels in the changing room, it can run into thousands of pounds. But what happens if, as we have discovered to our considerable cost recently, there's a global pandemic? You can't play golf and nor can you claim a refund. An extended lockdown, in effect, costs you a considerable sum of money but not if you have taken out a pandemic policy.

Someone who has shelled out, say, £2000 on his annual golf club membership surely won't baulk at paying a modest £100 on top to insure himself against not being able to play because of some nasty virus. It will be hugely profitable not only because these things only occur on average about once a century but also because, as we all know, you boys are hugely adept at finding reasons for not paying out. You could, for example shove a clause in the small print that says, inter alia, that you're only liable if the lockdown lasts for more than three months, which is most unlikely, and the first two months aren't covered anyway. Kerching!

All I ask is for a modest 10% commission on all the premiums. Interested?

Dear Professional Golfers Association of America,

I appreciate that in some energetic sports a build-up of phlegm in the mouth can occur that, where the individual concerned is reluctant to swallow aforementioned unpleasant substance, he or she may feel it necessary to spit. However, even when played quite quickly, which is, sadly, never the case in your events, golf isn't one of those sports and it is therefore complete unnecessary for the participants to do it. And so why do they do it, especially when millions of people all over the world are watching? What sort of example is that setting children? During the final round of the USPGA this year, I counted no fewer than seven, full-blown gobs, as we call them in the UK. Tiger Woods, Dustin Johnson... the bigger the name, the more it seems they feel the need to spit.

Although I don't want to make too big a thing of it, it's dramatically less prevalent among European golfers. For example, I've never seen Justin Rose, Rory McIlroy or even the slightly wild Tommy Fleetwood indulge in this disgusting practice so there is evidently a cultural element involved here. Having thought long and hard about the subject, I have rejected the idea of installing spittoons next to each tee and green as this would add unsightly clutter. Instead, I have come to the conclusion there is no alternative but to penalise players: one shot if the offence takes place on the tee, fairway or in the rough; two on the green and three if anyone is audacious enough to gob into the hole. That would pretty soon put a stop to it!

As I suspect you will be too pusillanimous for such decisive action, I have an alternative proposal. The scorers who accompany each group in the majors should be tasked with the responsibility of noting down every time a player spits. Then, at the end of the tournament, the 'winner' could be presented with the 'Silver Spitoon'; in other words, publicly humiliated.

Dear St George's Hill,

Those of us who love sport appreciate what a marvellously civilizing influence it can be. There are so many lessons that sport can teach us; self-discipline, magnanimity, confidence, graciousness, getting along with team-mates and accepting decisions. And there really is nothing like the delicious pleasure of crushing opponents, is there?

'Sport in the Community' deals with what are commonly termed 'problem children'. Almost exclusively from deprived backgrounds, they are simply kids who, through no fault of their own, find themselves at odds with society. Mostly they are just petty criminals who thieve and deal in drugs because they've never been shown a better way. Frequently disowned by their families and shunned by society, there's a real danger they will be consigned to life's waste-bin unless something dramatic is done to encourage them to mend their ways and change their lives.

Those of us involved in 'Sport in the Community' passionately believe we can rescue these children through sport. With responsibility for most of south-east London, I have so far managed to persuade various providers of sporting facilities to contribute at least some time to our youngsters. They include a ten-pin bowling alley, roller-skating rink, gym and swimming pool. Having identified golf as a suitable activity, I'm very much hoping you will be willing to help as well.

All we ask is that our boys and girls are welcomed at your club on, say, one or two days a week – preferably including a Saturday and/or Sunday – and are made to feel at home. Although to the best of my knowledge none has played golf before, most are willing to experiment and give it a go. If you could lend them the sticks and balls, I'm sure they would be happy to take it from there. We wouldn't presume to ask that you supervise them but it might be as well to keep a general eye on proceedings. It would, of course, be wonderful if we discovered the next Mick Faldo but I'm much more concerned that our kids learn that success has to be earned; a lesson I hope they will learn observing and mixing with your high achieving members.

****

Dear Prostatitis Sufferers' Association,

Normally large is a good thing. For example, a large portion of chips is better than a small portion, unless you're trying to lose weight, of course. But an enlarged prostate is, as we all know, really bad news as, apart from any other considerations, it means you have to wee far more often than non-sufferers.

Life can become awkward and embarrassing. One tip you might care to pass on to your members is only wear dark trousers; the darker the better. But it's with regard to sport in general and golf in particular that I'm writing to you now. Not unnaturally, men with prostatitis want to live as normal a life as possible and that includes participating in sport. But not all sports are prostatically friendly, so to speak. Take athletics, for example. Some events are clearly not as inclusive as they should be and, in effect, discriminate against those with enlarged prostates. The 10,000 metres can take well over half an hour, particularly if you're a bit slow. And that might be just too long for some. So why not persuade the athletic authorities to pause the race half-way so that those that need to can go to the toilet.

Tennis has been leading the way in this regard by allowing players to more or less go to the loo whenever they want. Sadly this progressive policy has led to a fair bit of abuse where players claim to need the toilet but are just leaving the court to break their opponent's concentration. I would suggest to the LTA and ATP that they should furnish each player with a sample jar that has to be filled by those requesting a break. Failure to fill it should cost offenders at least a set.

The only sport that really caters for prostatitis' sufferers is golf. Even though a round can take upwards of four hours, there are innumerable opportunities for players to relieve themselves in the trees and bushes. Links courses, which are in any case hugely over-rated and frequently prohibitively expensive, offer little cover in this regard and are therefore best avoided.

In conclusion, therefore, I would urge you to adopt golf as the official sport of the Prostatitis Sufferers' Association

Section 2

Hugely Controversial

Dear Penguin,

Love him or hate him, undoubtedly one of the most influential characters of the last century was Adolf Hitler. There have, I know, been an awful lot of books about him but none so far has explored what I think was a critical influence on him ... golf. My book, "Golf and the Rise of Fascism", examines the psychologically damaging effect of frequent defeats at Munich Municipal golf course at the hands of a number of Jewish players, principally Sol Sternberg, Moshe Levinsky and Abe Horowitz.

Unflinchingly honest, my book examines in some detail Hitler's strong grip which caused him to hook the ball, especially off the tee, much to the amusement of Steinberg, Levinsky and Horowitz. Their laughter and Hitler's embarrassment fuelled a sense of grievance that led first to his giving up the game and then, by stages, to the Second World War and the Holocaust.

Among the many issues explored in the book is the role of Uwe Pretzel, the assistant pro at the Munich course. Had he, the book speculates, persuaded Hitler to move the thumb on his right hand further round the shaft thereby weakening the grip, maybe the Second World War would have been avoided and over 20 million lives spared.

Painstakingly researched, the book includes observations from, amongst others, Albert Speer, Field Marshall Rommel and Arnold Palmer. Particularly revealing are some comments made by former President Roosevelt, who notes how any reference to golf in the diplomatic exchanges with Hitler met with a frosty response.

Prime Minister Neville Chamberlain made the mistake of inviting Hitler to play in a fourball partnering Goering against himself and Lord Halifax at Wentworth. Hitler couldn't be tempted, not even when Chamberlain suggested Poland as a side-stake. When the Prime Minister accused

the German Chancellor of being a "scaredy-cat", Hitler went into a rage, slammed his putter onto the cabinet table and vowed to "play through" Poland as if it were a "single player with no standing".
Would you be interested in publishing my book?

****

Dear Prince Andrew

First of all, thank you for the good work you're doing promoting golf. Too often the game is regarded by the general public as an elitist game that is the sole preserve of toffs, but you've done a great job demonstrating to the masses that everyone can play.
My purpose in writing is to ask you how a golf club goes about the business of having 'Royal' added to its name. I presume that someone royal like you has to come down to inspect the place and pass it as suitable for Royals generally. Is that right?
If there's an application form that has to be completed perhaps you would be kind enough to get one of your staff to post it to me.
The other thing of course is how much does it cost? Is there a one-off joining fee and then an annual subscription or what?
Finally, would it matter if the course only had nine holes?
The people I've spoken to at my club are all agreed that it's a great idea and that it would considerably enhance our reputation, both in the area and nationally, as well as boost our green fee revenue thus helping to keep our subscriptions down.

By the way, if you were able to help us, we would be both honoured and privileged to offer you free lifetime membership, a club tie and possibly a reserved space in the car park. Can you imagine how good it would look if there was a sign that read: "Reserved for HRH The Duke of York." That should be worth a couple of quid on the green fee, eh?
Now that you're not opening fetes, visiting hospitals, dishing out medals and all that nonsense, presumably you've got plenty of time to work on your swing. And you might like to know there's a couple of cracking young girls working in the pro shop who I'm sure you're going to like.

****

Dear Nigel Farrage,

I don't blame you for the appalling mess Brexit turned into because I don't suspect you had any idea when you were out there on the hustings whipping up xenophobia that it would degenerate into such a complete fiasco.
Even if the economy is wrecked, millions lose their jobs and we struggle to find the resources to do all the things we want to do for the NHS, education and social welfare, I'm sure we will all be a lot happier without any interference from abroad. Anyway, I'm writing to you now because I fear that in your understandable eagerness to distort the facts and generally dissemble, you may have overlooked an important area of human endeavour where dastardly Europeans may yet cause more havoc.
Because I lack your enormous self-confidence, which some say borders on supreme arrogance, I can't be certain but I believe golf's Ryder Cup is unique in fielding a team that represents Europe. Since it has not only enjoyed

considerable success in the biennial matches against the USA but has also fostered a tremendous camaraderie amongst players of different nationalities, I presume you will want to put a stop to it as it risks undermining the distrust and mutual suspicion that are such important elements of your xenophobic philosophy.

You should therefore be made aware that the next proposed Ryder Cup match is fast approaching, which means there's not a great deal of time for you to put a stop to it. Inevitably, millions of golf fans will be disappointed, but I assume you will think that a small price to pay for pursuing your goal of isolating us as far as is possible from the rest of Europe. To help stifle the inevitable outcry, you could explain that you're merely restoring the Ryder Cup to what it was pre-1978 when it was a Great Britain and Ireland team that took on the USA. I don't imagine for a moment that the fact we hardly ever won will bother you in the slightest.

****

Dear Head of Bombing, 48th Fighter Wing, RAF,

I'm considering building a brand-new golf course and have an option to purchase what is presently a sheep farm on Romney Marsh, Kent. However, I'll need some help and that is why I'm writing to you.

The 150-acre farm is ideal for golf in every respect other than it is almost completely flat. Although flatness might be a significant advantage in an airfield, it is quite definitely a disadvantage in a golf course.

I've looked at the landscaping option and, frankly, it is simply too costly to move hundreds of tons of earth about. It was whilst watching 'Apocalypse Now' that the idea came to me. Presumably you are always looking for new areas on which to practice your bombing. So, how about dropping a few cluster bombs and daisy cutters on my proposed golf course? Although it would be nice if they could be precisely targeted to create, for example, suitable greenside bunkers, frankly it wouldn't matter too much where they landed, provided of course that they didn't stray onto the nearby housing estate or main road as collateral damage is probably best avoided.

In return for your help, I'm happy to offer the pilots who actually drop the bombs complimentary membership of my club and all other USAF and RAF personnel, 50 per cent off the usual green fee.

Dear Supreme Leader of North Korea (can I call you Kim?),

When you were growing up, wasn't it a bit confusing having the same first name as your father? If your mother shouted, "Kim, would you keep the noise down as I'm trying to watch television?" would you immediately know who she was addressing? And that hyphen in your surname is rather exotic. Here in the UK, it used to be that only the aristocracy had hyphens, but nowadays it seems more prevalent among black footballers than it is among toffs.

Anyway, I'm writing to you about a subject that I know is close to your heart – world peace. Like you, I'm a great believer in it and believe I have found a way to turn it from a dream into reality. From my experience of playing golf for more than 40 years, I appreciate what a great opportunity it presents to make new friends and discuss things in a relaxed and calm environment.

Your dad, of course, was evidently a natural at the game and shot the proverbial lights out in the first round he ever played. Even if the six holes in one are possibly a slight exaggeration and, for argument's sake, he only had five, it's still sensational stuff. Thirty-eight under par is, quite frankly, incredible scoring.

My idea is for you to host a huge golf tournament (The Kim Classic?) on the Pyongyang course. Apart from anything else, an event such as this will help promote North Korea as a holiday destination. Instead of pros, you could invite world leaders to participate, nearly all of whom play golf, albeit not as well as your old man.

I would suggest a maximum of 72 players, a Stableford format (which should speed up play) and a complimentary bar. To mix things up a bit and reduce the risk of inadvertently aggravating an old border dispute, you could endeavour to go for a geographical spread and put, for example, a European prime minister in with an African tribal chief, a South American dictator and an Asian despot. Selling the valuable TV rights to, say, Amazon Prime should generate sufficient revenue to pay for at least half-a-dozen rockets.

****

Dear Secretary of Royal St George's,

I am a film producer who would very much like to use your famous clubhouse and course for a movie that is presently in what we call the development stage. At the moment, we're working on a script and preparing budgets and I'm hoping that you might be willing to help.

To be absolutely honest with you, the film is not the sort you're likely to see at your local cinema. But there again that sort doesn't often make money. Ours is what is popularly termed an 'adult movie' and distribution will be by mail order and through specialised outlets only.

With the working title "Confessions of a Golf Pro", it tells the story of a rather handsome golf professional who seduces his female pupils and most of the women's section at his club. He also employs two gorgeous Swedish assistants who keep the club members happy. As luck would have it, the pro-shop backs onto the men's showers, which makes life exciting for everyone.

The climax of the film, if that's a suitable term, comes when the golf pro is caught in bed with the captain's wife and the captain is similarly embarrassed when he's discovered in a bunker with one of the assistant pros by the club secretary, whose wife is next door having it away on the snooker table with the head greenkeeper.

Although there's a lot of sex and a fair bit of nudity, it's essentially a comedy that belongs somewhere in the 'Carry On' tradition. Assuming you're happy for us to use your facilities - it would only be for three or four days in the summer - because budgets are necessarily tight, we would rather have some sort of contra deal than pay for the facility. In return for letting us use your clubhouse, I'm prepared to offer your members a unique opportunity to star in the film as extras and receive a complimentary DVD copy of it.

It might also be possible to hold the premiere at your club and invite all your members to attend. In view of the subject matter, it might be as well not to invite wives and girlfriends. Royal St George's will also be acknowledged in the film's end credits. For your information, the total crew including cameras, lighting, sound, makeup, director, actors and actresses should number no more than 30.

Are you 'up' for it?

****

Dear Jeremy Corbyn,

Although it's quite likely that you perceive golf as a rather bourgeois activity, nevertheless I sense you would welcome an opportunity to metaphorically smack a seven-iron against the backside of all Zionists, Israelis and Jews. Harold Wilson, one of your predecessors of course, was a very keen golfer and a member of Hampstead Golf Club, which is quite near your home in upmarket Islington. I believe he left the club in protest against their policy of not admitting Jews, which doubtless you would regard as something of a plus!

Even if you don't follow the game closely, you will have no doubt heard of the British Open Golf Championship, which has been going even longer than the Labour Party. But did you know that ever since the first Open was held in 1860, it has never been won by a Palestinian? And I think we all know who is to blame for that – yes, Israel of course. Quite simply, very few Palestinians play golf because there are no courses for them to play on. Why, when the terrain, particularly around the sand dunes in Gaza, is ideally suited to golf? There's not even a nine-holer! Again, Israel is to blame because it has done absolutely nothing to encourage Palestinians to take up the game. What is Israel frightened of? That they will use the bunkers for military purposes? Or that they will thump long drives over the border fence without shouting 'fore' thereby threatening Israel's security?

Anti-Semites throughout the UK are looking to you, Jeremy, to highlight the appalling apartheid that exists between golfers and non-golfers in the Middle East and, of course, to blame Israel for absolutely everything that's wrong in the world.

****

Dear League Against Cruel Sports,

I'm not sure if golf is on your list of cruel sports. If it isn't, it certainly should be.

It would be hard for me to overestimate the enormous amount of psychological damage that golf has inflicted on me. Formerly a calm and placid person, I'm now irritable and twitchy.

The unrelenting mental pressure starts on the first tee when you have to drive off in front of a whole load of strangers and doesn't stop until you've attempted to hole a testing, six-foot, downhill putt with a touch of left to right break to halve the match on the 18th.

Then there are all manner of other horrors that can strike at any time and are perfectly capable of reducing even the toughest of grown men to a gibbering wreck. I hate to even think it, let alone, type the dreaded word ... shank, aaaaaaaaaarrrrgggghhhhhhh!

If you don't play the game you will almost certainly be unfamiliar with the most awful shot in golf, which flies off the clubface at the most appalling of angles. The worst thing is that it can strike anyone at any time. And after it has happened once, you know that it can happen again. Consequently, every shot thereafter is an ordeal. And God forbid if it does happen again, then you're as good as dead. And then there's putting and the dreaded yips... yeeeeeeeeeeeeeeekkkkkksssssss!

In case you don't know, the yips are an involuntary muscle spasm that twitches the putter head in your hand and causes you to miss comparatively short putts by embarrassingly huge distances. I've seen grown men reduced to tears and almost driven to suicide by this appalling affliction. As well as the psychological damage, golf can also ruin a perfectly good back and a perfectly good marriage.

Frankly foxhunting, hare coursing, and stag hunting, although somewhat messy, are comparatively benign activities. At least they only harm animals.

I'm planning a protest demonstration outside the main entrance at the next Open Championship. However, many people you're able to send in support would be most welcome. And so please hurry up and add golf to your list of cruel sports.

Dear Pope Francis,

Let me make myself clear from the outset, I'm not Roman Catholic. Apart from anything else, my dodgy hip makes it difficult for me to kneel, which would render praying rather problematic. And praying is clearly an important part of your religion. Not that I would be required to do anything about it unless I had ambitions to be a monk, celibacy is something else which, frankly, has little or no appeal. Although, as I say, Catholicism doesn't grab me by the cassock, so to speak, I remain open-minded about religion generally and could possibly be persuaded to join your lot if it could be demonstrated to work. Doubtless that sounds a bit unreasonable to someone like you who obviously has enormous faith, but I'm a practical and pragmatic man who needs concrete evidence that a thing works before I'm prepared to give up my Sunday mornings to sit on an uncomfortable bench in a an absurdly spacious and draughty building. Those candles don't give off a great deal of heat, do they?

What, you might reasonably ask, is it that I do on a Sunday morning that's more important than saving my soul? Well, unless it's raining, I would ordinarily be playing golf at Dale Hill Hotel and Golf Club, which is just to the south-east of Tunbridge Wells. I don't know whether it's the close proximity of nature or just the sheer fun of it all but, curiously, I believe there is a spiritual aspect to golf that undoubtedly has a religious dimension, although not perhaps in a conventional way. How else do you explain my friend Harry's ridiculous hole-in-one where the ball hit two trees and a waste-paper bin on its way into the hole? Harry, who was 78, had been playing golf for over 50 years and never had a hole-in-one before, died two days later. At last he was at peace.

Now to the main point of my letter. My putting has completely gone to pieces. I shan't try and explain the

'yips' to someone who doesn't play golf and is too preoccupied looking after the welfare of an estimated 1.2 billion people to worry too much about a poor 19 handicapper for whom three-putting is an enormous source of anguish, but it's a nightmare. The club pro hasn't been much help and so, forgive me asking, but do you know of a prayer that could sort it out? Or do you think, say, dipping my putter head in holy water might do the trick? Last question; is there a patron saint of golfers to whom I could appeal or stick a replica of him on my golf bag?
If you are able to help and my handicap drops below, say, 15, I promise to convert.

He did, he just prayed to end a golfer's Yips problem...

Section 3

Simply Preposterous

Dear Ewen Murray,

Forgive me writing to you as I've no doubt you're being approached the whole time by people wanting you to play at their club, open fetes or support their charity. Well, I've got a proposal that I believe will make me rich and you even richer.

As a nuclear physicist with a background in engineering, I'm peculiarly well qualified to conduct research into golf club design and construction. For the past four years I've been working on a revolutionary putter that tests have confirmed is five times more likely to hole a putt than a conventional putter. Unbelievable, I know, but true.

My handicap has tumbled from 19 to 10 in the 12 months I've been testing my new 'Krypton' putter. Why have I improved so much? Look at the stats. I'm hitting no more fairways than before (averaging 3.2 a round), reaching no more greens in regulation (2.8 a round) or registering more sand saves (lifetime average seemingly stuck on 0.27%) but I now regularly take fewer than 23 putts a round (my record is an astonishing 19!).

Working at a Ministry of Defence research laboratory gives me access to material and facilities denied to civilians. Anyway, all conventional putters are primarily reliant on good balance. You might be surprised to learn that mine isn't. All it does is literally impart a massive positive charge that effectively magnetises the ball so when it approaches or passes near the hole, it is attracted to the negative charge in the metal of the cup and is pulled towards it until it inevitably disappears into it.

Field tests have highlighted just a couple of minor problems that I feel obliged to disclose to you. Firstly, as it has an even stronger electrostatic field than the cup, the flagstick has to be removed well away otherwise the ball may adhere to it and be virtually impossible to remove. Secondly, there is a slight health and safety issue due to the depleted uranium core that is in the putter head. However, using a putter-cover impregnated with copper and a lead-lined golf bag, significantly reduces radiation levels. Mind you, finding a caddy who can lift a 225-pound golf bag can be a challenge.

In return for a modest percentage of the profits, would you be willing to endorse the 'Krypton' and mention it on Sky every time you get the chance?

****

Dear St Andrews,

I am reliably informed that the British Open will be played on the Old Course next year (2022), which I think will give you sufficient time to instigate the improvements outlined below.

Although St Andrews is undoubtedly steeped in history, what strikes me most of all whenever I watch golf being played there on TV is how featureless it is compared to the great American courses like Augusta National and Pebble Beach. Frankly, it's rather dull and so what can be done to improve it? It came to me like a well-struck seven-iron. What's the most important hole on a golf course? Why, the 18th of course, the finishing hole. So, perversely, this is where I suggest you start.

At the moment it's a rather uninteresting, short, par four. Goodness me, it's almost driveable! The Swilken Burn doesn't present enough of a hazard to worry the better players and, let's face it, most of the guys teeing it up at the British Open are more than averagely good. So what you must do is dam up the Swilken Burn and let the water flood the surrounding area until you've got a decent lake. It's a shame that the pretty stone bridge will be lost but you can easily find an alternative spot to dump it somewhere on the course. Or you might prefer to flog it to some rich Yank such as Donald Trump and the proceeds would help pay for the landscaping.

A nice big lake would make the competitors think more carefully on the tee. The trouble with the hole at present is that nothing very exciting ever happens apart from some poor geezer missing a short putt.

To top it all off tastefully and provide some visual interest, I suggest you install a really big fountain. A statue in the middle of, say, an old man stooped under the weight of his bag could be very effective, especially if there were jets of water streaming out of his clubs and into the sky. And a few Koi carp in the lake wouldn't do any harm either. They're not cheap but if you can persuade visitors that their golfing luck will improve if they empty their pockets into the lake, the fish will pay for themselves in no time.

The St Andrews fountain could become the most famous fountain in the whole of golf, which you might care to use for branding identity purposes on your merchandise.

Since I've probably given you enough to think about for now, I'll leave my idea on how to divide those ridiculous double greens with the careful use of Leylandii hedging for another time.

Dear TaylorMade,

Once a gifted 17 handicapper who was solid both off the tee and around the greens, I'm now struggling to break 100. Why? To put it bluntly, my body is letting me down. More specifically, it's my left hip. Arthritis has taken its toll and the nice people at my local hospital are now telling me that I need to replace it, presumably with a shiny new one, which is where you come in.

Instead of any old 'off-the-shelf' hip, I'd like a customised one specifically designed to, yes, improve my golf! Why, I thought to myself as I sat in the hospital waiting-room, can't my hip match my clubs? If I can play with forged-iron, cavity-back clubs, why can't I walk on a similarly designed hip with the same level of performance and forgiving properties? If, for example, my hip had the same coefficient of restitution as my driver, is it not reasonable to assume that I could sit down, get up and walk around with the same assuredness with which I drive it off the tee? And a graphite shaft connecting my hip to my femur should ensure I recover the sort of flexibility my body enjoyed 30 years ago. And what a psychological boost it would be to know that my hip and clubs were not only totally compatible but were manufactured by the very same people.

I appreciate that producing body parts is not an area into which you have ventured but, given the worrying decline in the number of people playing golf, wouldn't it be sensible to diversify? I'm sure all those white-coated boffins you presently employ to expand the sweet-spot, could easily turn their educated hands to reducing human suffering whilst at the same time rescuing veteran golfers from the indignity of a 20+ handicap.

If it encourages you to take up my suggestion, I would happily let you fit me with the very first TaylorMade hip in the world and have my game monitored to see what, if any, improvements followed.

Although I'm not sure whether or not you could sell them in pro shops, I am absolutely certain that artificial hips are a booming market that will surely continue to expand as the population ages.

Dear Hassan Rouhani,

I'm not a Muslim and therefore don't really understand, a) what the difference is between the Sunnis and Shiahs, or b) why you appear to be at each other's throats the whole time. To an outsider it seems crazy that one lot of Muslims doesn't get on with another lot. Presumably, as is often the case, there was an incident some while ago that caused a bit of ill-feeling and no one can bring themselves to apologise and say sorry. I had an Uncle Alf who fell out with my Auntie Gladys during a game of bridge because she bid three spades when she should have passed. To my knowledge, they never spoke to each other again. How silly is that?

Well, my suspicion is that your spat with the Shias is equally daft and could easily be resolved with a bit of goodwill on both sides. The problem often is that, fearing loss of face, neither side wants to make the first move. So let me be the one to propose something that could start the blessed process of reconciliation.

Sport unites where politics divides. So, rather than shouting, politicians should be playing. My suggestion is that the Sunnies and Shiahs should have an annual golf match alternately in Iran and, say, Saudi Arabia. Although I know the latter are building several decent courses I have no idea whether there are any suitable tracks in Iran. If I may say, it's not really my fault I don't know as you are rather a secretive lot. aren't you? Take nuclear weapons for example. Although everyone suspects you're building them, no one knows for certain because you seem keen to conceal stuff. Anyway, it could be that you regard golf as a decadent imperialist game. If that's the case, you're completely wrong. Just take a look at China and all the courses they're building there.

Back to the match. I suggest you start modestly with just one fourball; you and a friend against, say, King Abdullah and one of his (many) sons. If that goes well, you could gradually expand it to maybe a dozen a side. Then, who knows, you could copy the Ryder Cup format of foursomes, fourballs and singles over three days. Sky television might be interested in covering the event and, before you know it, a whole generation of young Sunnies and Shias will grow up thinking that they just belong to two opposing golf teams rather than implacably hostile enemies.

One final nice touch you might want to consider is inviting Israelis to referee the matches. In that way, you'd be taking another virtuous stride in the direction of world peace.

****

Dear Dr Ping,

You will be thrilled to learn that I have one of your putters. I got it cheap on eBay but am delighted with it. Every so often it seems to miss a bit on the right-hand side but, to be honest, it could very well be my fault and not the putter's. I'm writing because I've had what I think is a very good idea and would be interested to hear what you think of it. To take advantage of the twilight rate at my local course, I frequently tee off in the early evening. The place is blissfully quiet and the only downside is the light frequently fails towards the end of the round. Because I don't drive the ball very far, the poor visibility is less of a problem on the tee than it is on the green. I find reading the line of the putts increasingly difficult as the sun sinks while my putts don't. But, rather than moan, I've done something about it.

It's very simple really as it's essentially nothing much more than a torch that can be easily attached to the shaft of the putter. To distribute the weight more evenly, I've located the battery in the grip with a wire doing down the interior of the shaft. Incidentally, the same battery supplies power to a small coil heater that keeps the grip warm on a cold evening.

The torch is adjustable, as is the beam, so that I can illuminate a specific spot either on the line of the putt or on the hole itself. As a courtesy to my opponents, I always turn it off when they're putting. It really works incredibly well and the only negative is that it attracts annoying moths that can be an unwanted distraction and so I'm presently developing a device that emits a high-pitched screech that I'm hoping will scare them off.

My idea is to sell the kit that would enable golfers to convert their existing putters. All customers would need is a power drill, soldering iron and rudimentary knowledge of applied electro-physics. I'm hoping you will be willing to endorse my product along the lines of: "As recommended by Dr Ping."

****

GCSE-Level Examination – submitted to the Qualifications and Curriculum Authority

I'm encouraged that modern education extends beyond the three R's and that children are leaving school with a broader understanding of the world. However, there is one vital area of human activity that is still largely being ignored... golf. I believe the Royal and Ancient game is a legitimate area of study and should be included in the national curriculum. So, in a bid to start the ball rolling, so to speak, I've drafted a dummy GCSE level golf examination paper that will give you a good idea of what I'm about. Perhaps have a go at it yourself and let me know what you think.

Golf (Theory) GCSE Examination.

Although this paper should take no more than three-and-a-half hours to complete, it will probably take longer.

Candidates should be aware that if they fall more than one question behind the candidate in front of them, they should call through whoever is sitting behind.
Write an essay on one of the following:

1. Ben Hogan has a better swing than Nick Faldo but the Englishman wore more interesting sweaters. Discuss.
Or
Was what happened in the Ryder Cup at Brooklyn, Massachusetts, an indictment of matchplay golf or simply a few boozed up Yanks misbehaving themselves?
Or
Golfers have no dress sense. Discuss

2. Match up the golfers in column **A** with the most appropriate description in column **B**.

A)	B)
Tommy Fleetwood	God-fearing
Bernard Langer	Pissed
Bryson DeChambeau	Phenomenally rich
Shane Lowry	A Nutter
Tiger Woods	Needs a haircut
Nick Faldo	Not Very Popular
John Daly	Should go on a diet

3. Your ball lands in a cowpat. Do you:
a) Claim relief, on the basis that playing it as it lies is just too disgusting?

b) Nudge it away gently with your shoe when your playing partners aren't looking? or
c) Drop it under penalty of one stroke?

4. A member of your regular fourball never buys a round of drinks. Without recourse to physical violence, explain how you would deal with the situation.

5. Which is the odd one out and why?
St Andrews, Royal Troon, Carnoustie, Royal Birkdale, Royal St. George's and Dale Hill Hotel and Golf Club

6. Your club car park is full except for the space reserved for the Captain. Do you a) Find somewhere else to park? b) Reverse into the Captain's spot and accidentally knock down the sign so that you can claim that you didn't realize it was his? or c) Park alongside the 18th green by way of protest at the inadequate parking provision and be prepared to join another club?

7. Using diagrams, explain what happens when you shank a ball.

****

Dear Mr Callaway,

Golf equipment is, I know, a very competitive business. Because the only thing that matters to the overwhelming majority of golfers is smashing the ball further, this rivalry must be particularly acute when it comes to drivers. Irons are all very well and wedges certainly have their place but I suspect the driver is the flagship in your fleet. If you can outgun the opposition, then you're well on the way to the top of the pile and I'm certain I can help you achieve that.

Ever since I was a young lad, I've been interested in explosives. As a boy, I would take fireworks apart and then put them back together so that they behaved differently to the way the manufacturers intended. I would change the colours around, make rockets fly further and increase the decibel level of the bangs. This background in explosives has helped me in my recent quest to develop a driver that will really hit the ball immense distances, and I mean IMMENSE.

You'll understand, I know, that for commercial reasons I'm not in a position to reveal the details but I have developed a club I call the 'Howitzer' that consistently hits the ball comfortably over 400 yards. My record to date on flat terrain with no following wind is 518 yards. Imagine driving the green on a par five! And the best thing about it is that anyone can achieve these distances because club head speed is almost totally irrelevant.

As with all new technology there are one or two teething problems. The principal headache, and I choose the word advisedly, that I'm wrestling with at the moment is the almost unbearable noise. Unsurprisingly, the club at impact sounds not unlike a very loud shotgun, which can be quite a problem when, as is often the case, the tee is adjacent to a green that may or may not have people putting on it.

The other challenge is trying to eliminate the near blinding flash that accompanies the bang. During trials, I've been wearing goggles and ear-muffs and there is clearly a commercial opportunity in selling these accessories along with the 'Howitzer'. Because there are so many conservative elements in the golfing establishment, I would be lying if I said everyone will welcome the 'Howitzer'. But you have experience of these and doubtless an expert legal department that will help you overcome these reactionary elements.

In conclusion, what I'm hoping for is some form of joint venture with you that married my technical genius with your considerable experience to our great mutual advantage.

****

Dear Boris Johnson,

I don't know whether or not you play golf but, either way, I'm certain you are going to like the incredible idea I've had.

It came to when riding upstairs on the 88 bus travelling along the Bayswater Road. Looking out at the enormous expanse of grass that is Hyde Park, it surprised me how few people there were enjoying this excellent facility. Then it struck me; what a wonderful opportunity exists for developing a truly, world-beating golf course right in the centre of the world's greatest city.

So excited was I by the idea that I immediately jumped off the bus and took a good look around. And the more I looked, the more excited I became. For example, the Serpentine could, with a little imagination and re-shaping, make a wonderful water feature guarding the green of a tricky par three.

Although I appreciate there are a few royals knocking about in Kensingon Palace, I'm sure they wouldn't mind being confined to, say, the top floor to enable the balance of the building to be converted into arguably the greatest and most historic clubhouse in the world. Possibly the only negative I can identify in the whole scheme is that there's no way to avoid felling a few old trees. But I would estimate no more than four or five hundred would need to go.

The big plus from both your and the Treasury's point of view would be the enormous income that would be generated. At present there's just the deckchair rental and a modest revenue from the Serpentine café but I'm talking tens of millions of pounds. Membership of the incredibly exclusive Royal Hyde Park Golf and Country Club (Patron: HM the Queen) would be hugely sought after by all those fat cats who live in Kensington, Belgravia and Knightsbridge. Even at half-a-million quid, I'm certain you would have no difficulty enrolling, say, 1000 members.

Then there are the corporates! How much do you think a Japanese bank would pay to join? Five million? The revenue would be fantastic and we've not even considered bar sales and the pro shop. And what about the worldwide merchandising possibilities? The income could make good your extravagant election promise to boost the NHS. And there would be enough left over to fund a significant tax cut in the next budget to satisfy your rich friends. Handled properly and provided your daft Brexit doesn't bugger everything up, it could on its own almost guarantee you another four years in the top job.

****

Dear Brother or Sister Chairperson of the Communist Party of Great Britain,

The last couple of decades have been pretty depressing for those of us who have been eagerly anticipating the imminent collapse of capitalism and the long awaited take over by the oppressed proletariat. On the other hand, the weather seems to be steadily improving and Spurs are still in the Premiership.

Although I'm completely confident that brother Karl more or less got it right when he predicted the inevitable demise of capitalism, I believe that the irresistible forces of history might need to be gently encouraged if this particular working-class hero is to be around to witness the revolution.

Somewhat weary of working within the system to bring about its collapse (I had a temporary job at my local newsagent and deliberately creased copies of the Daily Telegraph) I now recognise that there is no alternative to direct action. I believe the time is right to strike at the soft underbelly of capitalism and hit the exploiters where they gather in great numbers to orchestrate their oppression. I'm referring, of course, to golf clubs.

Although destroying all the clubhouses has considerable appeal, a more subtle approach might be less confrontational.

What I propose, therefore, is that we metaphorically tear down the symbols of power by moving to a distant corner of the car park all the spaces reserved for the Chairmen, Captains and Lady Captains. Apart from the enormous psychological impact to be gained from striking at the undemocratic symbols of elitism and power, the practical chaos that will be wrought when BMW, Mercedes, and other flash motors are ousted from their regular spaces will almost certainly throw the oppressors into disarray. At that moment, while they are all looking for somewhere to park, we'll move in and seize control of the means of production, the media and whatever else we need in order to liberate the masses.

****

Dear Thomas Bach, Chairman of the International Olympic Committee,

The Olympics are fast becoming one of the undoubted highlights of the sporting calendar, spanning so many different sports and involving so many athletes. It's too bad the winter Olympics have to take place in the winter but I don't suppose there is anything you can do about that. Anyway, the summer Olympics are unbelievably popular and have a global appeal that's right up there with the University Boat Race and Greyhound Derby.

However, as you know better than most it's fatal to become complacent and the Olympics must continually evolve if they are to maintain their pre-eminence. And so it was that I began thinking what I could do to improve things. Because of a personal worry I have about energy conservation and global warming, I wonder sometimes about the example being set by having the Olympic flame burning so extravagantly the whole time. I appreciate its symbolic importance but feel that it could at least be reduced in size or, better still, switched off between events. Another thing, is anyone really interested in dressage and synchronized swimming?

I'm so pleased you finally caved in to financial pressure from the likes of Nike, Titleist and Ping and re-instated golf. However, do we really need yet another 72-hole, strokeplay tournament that is hardly distinguishable from any other golf event?

So here's what I suggest. Each country that wishes to participate should enter a fourball team made up of a professional golfer, a businessman, a showbiz celebrity and a prominent politician. The US dream team, for example, could be made up of Tiger Woods, Bill Gates, Jack Nicholson and Donald Trump. Imagine both the enormous interest that would be generated and the opportunities it would create for world leaders to sort out their problems in a relaxed atmosphere over a pint of beer in the clubhouse afterwards.

The two best balls of the four to count and, because I don't doubt whether the celebrities and politicians have much stamina, it probably should be an 18-hole event.

****

Dear Messers Royal and Ancient,

First of all, may I congratulate you on a wonderful game. I took up golf just over 12 months ago and just love it. My wife says I spend more time at my club than I do with her. If you met her, you would understand why! Just kidding.

Anyway, my point it writing is not to make jokes at the expense of the old trouble and strife but to suggest how the game might be improved. Even with the reduction in the time allowed to look for balls, too many minutes are wasted thrashing around impenetrable undergrowth. Why? Because the 'shot and distance' rule is far too harsh. Instead, I think a player who has either lost a ball or can't be arsed to look for it should be allowed to drop another one more or less where he was aiming the original ball at the cost of just one shot. Also, escaping from bunkers is far too difficult for the ordinary man or woman, especially when the ball is in an awkward spot. Without penalty, I suggest a player be allowed to kick the ball just once in a bunker to a more reasonable position provided that it remains in the bunker. Where a player accidentally hits a ball out of bounds but there was no intent on his part to secure an advantage by, say, cutting a corner, he may play the shot again with no penalty. Since golf is an honourable game played by honourable men and women, the final decision as to whether there was intent or not rests solely with the player. Finally, to make putting both more exciting and fairer, a putt that lips out should count as one-and-a-half shots but the putt should be deemed to have been holed. For example, a player putting for a four whose ball lips out should score four-and-a-half not five. In matchplay, obviously four-and-a-half beats a five but in strokeplay all half shots are rounded up at the end to avoid awkward scores such as 104-and-a-half, which of course would count as 105.

****

Dear William Hill,

Not since Oxo won the Grand National quite a few years ago have I had a bet. However, I fancy a tickle on a forthcoming competition at Dale Hill Hotel and Golf Club, which is where I've been a member since 1986 but still haven't been invited to be club captain. Perhaps you can give me odds on that happening before I move on up to the Great Clubhouse in the Sky. Another time, perhaps.

The July Mid-Week Stableford is the competition I have in mind. It normally attracts a modest field that barely reaches double figures but that need not concern you as the somewhat complicated bet I have in mind has nothing do with the result.

As usual, I shall be playing with the same group I've played with every week for the past 27 years – Martin, Peter and Guy. I appreciate that I ought to make a greater effort to get to know more of the members but somehow can't be arsed. To be honest, although Guy's okay, the other two are incredibly dull. Martin moans the whole time about his arthritic hip while Peter has to be among the slowest golfers on the planet.

Anyway, I would like an accumulator on the following. To make it easier for you since you obviously don't know the people involved, I have inserted what I honestly consider are fair odds next to each leg of the bet. If you would like to conduct further research, I can let you have the mobile phone numbers of the other three so that you can chat to them and make up your own mind.

1)   Martin being the last to turn up   5/4
2)   Guy forgetting a pencil to mark the card   1/1
3)   My drive down the first being the longest in our group   2/1
4)   Me hitting the green on all four par threes   4/1
5)   Me not going into any bunker the entire round   5/2
6)   Me not three-putting at all   4/1
7)   Guy hitting at least one T-shot out of bounds   4/6
8)   Martin uttering at least two audible expletives on each nine   1/1
9)   Peter losing at least one ball on each nine   4/5
10)   My nett score being the lowest   11/4
11)   Peter offering to buy the first round of drinks   7/4

By my reckoning, but I think you should do your own calculation, the cumulative odds of all the above happening are 65,780 to one. If so, I should like to put the enclosed fiver on to win £328,904.

Finally, I noted in a recent promotion of yours that you were offering to return punters' stakes in the event of one leg of an accumulator going down. Is that still valid? In which case, if only 10 of the above 11, come good, do I get my fiver back?

Section 4

Utterly Ridiculous

Dear Head of Titleist,

Although I don't buy any, I'm always pleased if I find a Titleist so your advertising clearly works, even if it doesn't always necessarily result in increased sales. And it's about the issue of lost golf balls that I'm writing to you.
As an environmentalist, I'm rather concerned that they are polluting the planet. It's not your fault because it's not you who are losing them. However, as the manufacturer, I believe you have a social responsibility here. My worry is that your balls contain a number of toxic substances that contaminate both the soil and water, thereby harming mammals, fish, birds and even often forgotten insects.
Instead of simply complaining, I have come up with an environmentally friendly alternative. Called the Ecoball, it's made entirely of vegetable matter - mostly a blend of crushed walnut shells and shredded acorns. It's non-toxic and biodegradable.
Lost Ecoballs simply rot and, far from doing damage, actually enrich the soil. My research also shows that they are positively liked by certain species of fish, particularly carp, which eagerly feed on the decaying matter.
In a world of increasing environmental awareness I believe that there are a growing number of people, and golfers are not very different from ordinary people, who would willingly pay a small premium for a product that was environmentally benign.
The only significant drawbacks I've so far encountered with the Ecoball are: 1) Their tendency to dissolve in water renders them impractical in wet weather; 2) You can't leave them too long on a damp fairway whilst, for example, looking for your playing partner's ball, because they will start to take root; and 3) They travel a little under half the distance of a conventional ball. Regarding the last point, I believe responsible golfers would willingly trade a little length in return for not harming the planet, don't you?

Would you be interested in some form of joint venture, which combined your manufacturing and marketing might with my pioneering concept?

****

Dear Wentworth,

Three years ago, GLOVE was formed. It stands for Growing Lovely Organic Vegetables Everywhere. We have, appropriately, a five-point program that we believe will help combat the world food shortage, whilst at the same time doing no harm to the environment.

The first of these five points is to identify suitable sites for planting, growing and harvesting our vegetables. These sites can be anything from railway embankments and motorway verges to waste tips and roundabouts. They come in all shapes and sizes.

What they have in common is that they are otherwise unproductive. At our recent AGM, one of our Surrey members came up with an enormously interesting suggestion that we investigate the possibilities that exist on golf courses. She lives quite close to you and thought that you might be willing to help.

Although I don't play the game myself, I understand that the only important bits of the course are what you call the fairways and greens.

Apparently, there are substantial tracts of land elsewhere that are almost entirely unused. These I gather, are called the rough and strictly speaking shouldn't be visited by the players.

This is how GLOVE works. One of our people will survey your site, carry out soil tests and identify suitable areas. We will then draw up a planting program tailor-made for you.

Our people are trained to be unobtrusive but, so that you can readily identify them, they wear bright yellow overalls with a big red GLOVE logo on the back.

They will prepare the land, plant the seeds, tend to plants and harvest the crop. Because they are mostly volunteers who have regular jobs during the week, they'll mostly be on your course at weekends, which I assume would be best for you anyway.

Our intention is to inconvenience you as little as possible. In fact, you won't have to do anything. All we ask is that you desist from using any insecticides, weed killers or other chemical treatments within 400 yards of any of our plots. We would also appreciate it enormously if when you mow the fairways and greens that you pile the clippings onto a convenient compost heap. In return for your help, we are happy to give you 10% of everything we grow. Should you want more we'll gladly sell it to you at a 25% discount on our normal prices.

As we will need to move quickly if we are to get our parsnips established before the soil dries out, perhaps you would be kind enough to let me have a speedy response to this appeal.

****

Dear Early Man Department at the British Museum,

You may or may not be aware that there is some confusion and dispute about the origins of golf and in which country it was first played. The Scots would have you believe that they invented it, as would the Dutch, American Indians, Mongols, Greeks and many others. Considerable national prestige is the prize to be won by the country that can prove that it's the only true originator of the game.

All the above leads me on to a rather extraordinary find I made last month whilst playing in my club's midweek Stableford. Rather uncharacteristically for me, since I tend to draw the ball rather than fade it, I sliced my drive into the trees on the right of the fairway on the par four 14th. My suspicion is that I probably took the club back outside the line and failed to bring it back to square on impact.

Since the ball was a pretty decent one, I ventured into the woods in search of it. Although I never in fact found it, what I did discover was indeed quite remarkable.

First of all, there was a very old bone that had been fashioned into something akin to a lob wedge. There will, I know, be sceptics who will say that it is just an old bone that happens to resemble the shape of a golf club. However, close inspection of the top of the bone reveals heavy scratch marks. The significance of these is quite clear to me. If indeed what I found was an early, say Neolithic, golf club, it would have been used during a particularly wet period in the earth's history. Heavy rain will have rendered the club slippery and early man, without the benefit of modern all-weather grips, will have needed to improve adhesion by effectively roughing up the top of the club. This will have given him a competitive edge and, who knows, improved his chances of capturing the Club Championship and mating with whoever he chose from the women's section.

Before you dismiss this as pure speculation, you should examine the "ball" I found nearby. Although considerably heavier and with far fewer dimples than the modern equivalent and almost certainly less responsive around the green, it would undoubtedly have done the job.
It occurred to me that an ancient predecessor of mine might have entered the self-same wood, searching for his ball, some several thousand years earlier and been attacked by a sabre-toothed tiger.
Given the likely historical significance, I'm reluctant to post the objects. Would it be possible to bring them along and show them to an expert?

****

Dear American Golf,

Before I introduce you to my amazing invention, may I ask whose side you are on in the Ryder Cup? Your name suggests you support the Yanks. Is that right?
Never mind, my purpose in writing to you now is to introduce you to the incredible Pentapole which, as the name suggests, is five things in one; all of which every golfer should take with him or her onto the course.
Okay, you've hit you're opening tee shot into a fairway bunker. After you've knocked the ball back onto the fairway, there's a problem... no rake. Don't panic, simply pick up your Pentapole, flick the control to 'R' and out will pop a rake with a reach of just over two metres. Finished with it? Simply press 'R' again and the rake will withdraw back into the Pentapole.
As you wedge-it to the green, you take a significant divot which flies 10 feet in front of you. You don't have to walk forward to retrieve it and then back to replace it, just flick

the switch on your Pentapole to 'D' and a five-pronged, metal 'hand' will extend up to three metres, scoop up the divot and return it to you. Incidentally, the divot returner doubles as a ball retriever to recover wayward shots that, for example, plop into a water hazard or on the wrong side of a barbed-wire fence.

Your next tee shot lands three-quarters of the way up a hill and leaves you with a blind shot to the green. Is there anyone on the green? And where on the green is the flag? Don't trudge up the hill to look, just press 'P' on your Pentapole and an eight-metre long periscope will extend upwards to give you a clear sight of the green.

Now you're on the green and worried that the group behind, because they can't see you, might hit up and cause you injury at best and to miss the putt at worst. Press 'F' on the Pentapole control and the periscope will once again rise eight metres in the air but this time a red flag will spring out of it which emits a high-pitched alarm so you will be both visible and audible to the group behind.

Finally, as you stride up the 18th, a threatening cloud looms up behind the clubhouse. Could it be a thunderstorm? Don't panic, just press 'L' on your Pentapole control and a 15-metre lightning conductor will soar skyward. Plant it in the ground and then stroll to the clubhouse knowing that any lightning in the vicinity will strike it and not you.

Final point, don't forget to go back out and retrieve your Pentapole before driving home as they cost £99.99. Cheap for an item that saves you money and energy while protecting you from being struck both by other golfers and God. How many Pentapoles would you like to order for your shops?

Dear Armitage Shanks,

Like many with a handicap as high as mine, I get rather nervous before commencing a round of golf and almost invariably have to visit the gents. That in itself is not a problem but for the fact that your toiletware (is that the correct word?), which in all other respects is fine, causes me considerable anguish simply because of the name, 'Armitage Shanks'. Because it's displayed quite prominently on the urinals, doubtless for marketing purposes, I tried switching to the cubicles but there it was again on the toilet bowls. There really is no escaping it.

I have no problem with Armitage, which is indeed an elegant name, but 'Shanks' is very problematic for those, like me, who have an unhappy history of occasionally hitting golf balls almost sideways. In the UK we call that unmentionable shot a – I can hardly bring myself to type the word – shank ... aaaarrrrgggggghhhh!. It's horrible and incredibly destructive. It got so bad with me that I paid a fortune to see a sports psychologist who said I must obliterate all thoughts of it from my mind. How can I do that when your company's name screams out at me before I have even walked to the first tee? There are some bushes at the back of the car park but, although there's nothing in the Rules of Golf about it, old-fashioned golf clubs, and mine is one of those, frown on that sort of thing; if caught I could be suspended or even thrown out.

May I therefore respectfully urge you to re-brand your products in the UK. Having given it considerable thought, I believe I have an altogether better and more acceptable name. 'Flush' is a good positive word in golf that means to strike the ball perfectly. And, of course, it's appropriate to your industry. And so 'Armitage Flush' would ensure continuity whilst at the same time avoiding distressing anxious golfers like me.

Dear Golf Museum in St Andrews,

Because it was raining so heavily when I visited St Andrews in February (unusual for Scotland, eh?), I wasn't able to achieve my life's ambition of playing the Old Course and so I instead wandered around your museum. Although quite interesting, it was no substitute for the Road Hole or taking on the Swilken Burn. Never mind. Anyway, I have an idea for 'beefing' up your exhibits which I'm hoping you will like.
Next month I'm having my left hip replaced, which set me thinking. I have very little idea of what my left hip or, for that matter, my right hip, looks like. The same is true of the rest of my joints and all my internal organs. Since the purpose of museums is to educate and entertain, don't you think it would add enormously to the appeal of yours if you could display body parts in an attractive and interesting way?
Although I've not formally asked, I've no doubt the Conquest Hospital in Hastings would be happy to post you my old hip. However, I recognise that, despite the fact that I'm still the only member at Hendon Golf Club to have won three consecutive monthly mid-week Stableford competitions (1976 - September, October and November), my hip isn't of huge interest to many people. The same, I don't think, could be said of, say, Jon Daly's liver or Tiger Woods's back.
In the same way that we're all being asked to carry organ donor cards, perhaps you could persuade the top players to do something similar so, in the event of their death, you would have first dibs on their body parts. It may sound a bit grisly but it would be very educational.

Dear Sotheby's,

Because you hold regular auctions, you should be in a good position to advise what I should do with my tee pegs. If you don't play golf, you might not know that tee pegs are the little structures upon which you place your ball when teeing off.

Ever since I started playing golf back in the early 1970s I've collected them. Today I have somewhere in the region of 25,000.

My collection is held in over 100 shoe boxes and is filed according to material: 'wood', 'plastic', and 'other': by height: 'very tall', 'tall', 'moderately tall', 'average', 'below average', 'short' and 'very short': and by colour: 'red', 'blue', 'green', 'yellow', etc. So, for example, if I need a moderately tall yellow one made of plastic I know precisely in which box to look.

Some of the tee-pegs bear the names of companies and golf courses on the stem, while others are blank. Although I don't know, because I haven't been able to find any information anywhere, my suspicion is that my most valuable ones will be those bearing a company name that for whatever reason is not around anymore. For example, I have a few with "BCCI" on them, "Thames TV Golf Society", "Maxwell Communications", and my most prized one of all "Fly Concorde", although the last named is a bit damaged.

How do I go about selling them through your auction? Would they be auctioned individually or by the box, or do you think they would fetch more as a collection? Although I know it's difficult to say, do you have any idea what they might be worth?

Dear Head Greenkeeper of Royal Troon,

Like every other greenkeeper in the world, no doubt one of your biggest headaches is keeping your greens looking good and playing well. Members and visitors alike expect the greens to be smooth and true throughout the year and whatever the weather. Well, you will be thrilled to learn that your prayers have been answered and there's now a product that will both save you enormous amounts of money and provide the finest, truest greens in the world.

Although it looks and feels just like bentgrass, Omniturf has the enormous advantage in that it requires zero maintenance and is guaranteed to last for 25 years! Manufactured from a secret blend of some of the finest artificial fibres known to man, Omniturf behaves just like grass, looks just like grass and, thanks to our amazing boffins, even smells just like grass!

I'm sure you're now thinking this is just too good to be true. Well, what is even better is that we're willing to give – yes, GIVE – you a free demonstration. Here's the deal. Choose any one of your greens and, provided it's no bigger than 2500 square metres, we'll remove it and replace it with Omniturf to give you a chance to test if for yourself. The whole operation only takes a week.

We're extremely confident that after you've tried it, you'll want us to come back and do the lot. To give you some idea of cost, 18 average-sized greens generally works out at somewhere in the region of £1m. You'll probably save that in fertiliser, weedkiller and fungal treatments inside 24 months. And there's more money to be saved by firing most of the overpaid green staff and instead getting the comparatively cheap cleaners who look after the clubhouse to vacuum the greens about once a fortnight.

Dear Golf Equipment Wholesaler,

As distributors of golf equipment, you will appreciate the spectacular technological improvements that have been made in recent times. Titanium, graphite and other high tech materials have taken over from wood and steel.
Consequently, today's clubs and balls bear little resemblance to those our grandfathers used. Every facet of golf, including the bag, trolley and ball has undergone dramatic changes. Even the humble shoe spike has recently been transformed.
However, there is one tiny area where there has been absolutely no change at all. The tee-peg is precisely the same humble piece of wood it has always been. But I believe its days are numbered as I have developed the next generation of tee-peg.
Called the "Eternitee", it has a number of remarkable features that its predecessor lacks. Firstly, it is a precision piece of equipment that can set the ball at precisely the same height off the ground every time. Secondly, it has a memory that will adjust that height to whatever is appropriate for the club you're using.
Thirdly, since it sits on the ground rather than in it, it reduces club deceleration on impact. Finally, because of an audible signal it emits five seconds after the shot, and every five seconds thereafter, it simply can't be lost. Hence, "Eternitee".
It works like this. The telescopic stem is controlled by a small chip in the base. The cup is also the dial, which turns so the arrow points to the number of whichever club is being used. The peg is most extended for a driver and most retracted for a lob wedge.
One of the chief advantages it has over the present peg is that you only need one instead of a number at different heights. Also, being made of titanium and virtually

indestructible, you don't have to carry more than one in your pocket so no more embarrassing moments trying to locate your ball-marker in amongst a jumble of pegs.
Also worth mentioning is the fact that the battery is automatically recharged by the action of being struck. So, although at £49.99, it might seem expensive, it will last for years and save money in the long run.
Finally, by slashing the number of broken pegs littering the tees, it will help keep courses tidy whilst saving the planet by reducing waste.

****

Dear Lewis Hamilton,

As you know better than most, speed is a wonderful thing. And what impresses me about F1, even more than roaring down the straight at 200mph or thereabouts, is the speed with which they change your tyres. Compare the six or seven seconds they do it in with the one-and-a-half hours my local garage took to switch over my spare with the nearside front left about a fortnight ago.
Anyway, I gather you play golf and probably agree with me that it provides a far greater adrenaline rush than driving a car ever can. Going round and round the same circuit over and over again must be so dull that staying awake has to be a problem, surely. Whenever I feel a bit drowsy behind the wheel I switch on Radio 5 Live, which helps. Do you have a radio in your Mercedes or does all the clever technology take up so much space there's no room on the dashboard for the knobs?
Back to golf. For busy people like you and me, what we least like about the game is the inordinate amount of time it

takes to play a round. Part of the problem is, of course, slow play but I'm afraid there is not a lot we can do about that. However, there is one area which I believe offers enormous scope and that is the buggies. Why do they have to be so slow? Probably because they don't want you to know how slow they really are, there's no speedometer but I would be surprised if their top speed was more than about 10mph. If you could raise that to, say, 50mph, think how much time that would save.

Why don't you have a word with the technical team at Mercedes and persuade them to design a sort of F1 golf buggy. We could call it the 'Hurry-up Hamilton', flog it to golf clubs all over the world and become obscenely rich, if you're not that already.

****

Dear PGA of Europe,

Although the Ryder Cup is undoubtedly one of the outstanding sporting occasions ranking alongside such other iconic events such as the University Boat Race, the Grand National and the Eurovision Song Contest, I think it's beginning to get just a tiny bit out of hand. Remember Brookline?

It's no good just wringing our hands, we must do something about it. What I'm proposing is a number of minor modifications to the format that I'm confident will ensure the event's survival as a wonderful, international, sporting occasion whilst at the same time eliminating some of the less desirable aspects of it.

The problem, as I see it, is the matchplay format with its inherent confrontational character. Put two or four red-blooded blokes in a head-to-head game and, inevitably, aggression is generated which eventually turns unpleasant. Then the crowd gets involved and things get out of hand. I've seen it in WWE wrestling on Sky and I fear we will witness it at a forthcoming Ryder Cup unless something is done. Fortunately, it's not too late.

So here's what I propose. On day one, instead of foursomes in the morning and fourballs in the afternoon, I suggest we kick off with a long-driving competition. Unlike the existing arrangement where only some of the guys get to play on the first two days, all 24 players hit three balls. Each hits one ball in turn with the US and Europe going alternately. To make it easier for the spectators and TV, the two sides could hit differently coloured balls. Only one ball from each player to count with the longest hitting scoring 24 points and the shortest just one point.

Although I've not yet worked out all the details, other contests could include crazy putting, a nearest-the-pin competition, a Texas scramble, etc. Instead of three days of cut-throat matchplay, you would have three days of fun and games. Instead of harsh words and mutual recrimination, you would have happiness and laughter. And at the end, the winners will lift the trophy and the losers will have had a good time. Finally, let's hope the Yanks get stuffed!

Section 5

Pure Fantasy

Dear Augusta National,

You will recall the little Welshman who won the US Masters quite a while back, Ian Woosnam. Well, by extraordinary coincidence he designed one of the two courses at my club, Dale Hill Hotel and Golf Club in East Sussex, England. So, in a sense, our two clubs are already inextricably bound together. My hope is to further strengthen the bonds between us so that despite the fact that we are separated by a great ocean and little bits of land at either end, we may forge a partnership that will survive for centuries, and, incidentally, strengthen my bid for captaincy.

If I may explain that last bit. For some time now, I have felt that I should be elected captain at Dale Hill but, because of what I'm sure is nothing other than racial prejudice - something I'm sure Augusta National would never tolerate - I have been passed over. So I need to pull off an amazing coup, or something similar, to convince members that I should be captain.

May I suggest the following reciprocal arrangements as the first tentative couple of steps towards establishing closer ties between our clubs.

1) The winner of the US Masters be exempted from qualifying in the usual way for our biggest tournament, The Greenshield Trophy (a scratch competition ordinarily restricted to those who have won either a medal or Stableford competition in the previous 12 months). To even things up, I think The Greenshield Trophy winner should then automatically qualify for the following year's US Masters.

2) Both sets of members be offered the courtesy of the other's course so that Augusta National members visiting this country can play Dale Hill for nothing; while our members, who might find themselves in Augusta, can play your course for free. I feel compelled to warn you, however,

that you'll find our greens are pretty quick, especially in summer.

****

Chairman of The Open Championship Venue Selection Committee,

The British Open is undoubtedly one of the biggest events in the golfing calendar. However, I think there is a real danger of it becoming a bit stale. What do I mean? For example, it always seems to be held on a seaside course. These are pleasant enough and, watching the waves crashing on the shore, doubtless helps players relax. But what worries me is that foreigners watching on television will think Britain is no more than just a length of coastline. What about all the pretty inland courses? Why are they never chosen to host the event?

Take my own club Dale Hill Hotel and Golf Club, just south of Tunbridge Wells. Apart from the fact that they use builders' sand in the bunkers, what's wrong with it? It has what I believe they call "the necessary infrastructure", including a sauna and well stocked pro-shop.

Although the A21 is a bit slow in places, there's a 50-bedroom hotel which, assuming they are prepared to double up, could accommodate most of the field. There's a modest swimming pool, two dining rooms and a large selection of beers.

The carpark presently only holds about 200 vehicles but it could be extended if necessary around the back of the greenkeeper's shed. What's more, and this is where it has the edge over, say, Muirfield, it has two courses. Splitting the field would make life a lot easier for you and remove the need for ridiculously early tee off times.

I've spoken informally to the general manager and he has no objections in principle, although he didn't like the sound of a tented village "flattening the grass", so we may have to look at that one. And care would have to be taken regarding dates so as not to clash with one of Dale Hill's biggest events, the July Cup. However, with goodwill on both sides, I see no reason why these obstacles can't be overcome.

Bringing the British Open to this part of East Sussex will not only provide the local economy with a much-needed boost, I believe it will also refresh what is in danger of becoming a rather tired tournament and give the pros an exciting new challenge. Is it too late for next year?

****

Dear Roland McDonald,

Rather than try and fight this vegan thing, I would urge you to embrace it as you would a wounded cauliflower. Although vegetables aren't anywhere near as tasty as lovely meat, undoubtedly there is scope for producing dishes which are borderline edible. Combining my love for the great game of golf with a passion for cooking, I believe I have come up with something that will both appeal to your many customers as well as encourage them to take up golf. To answer your anticipated question as to why McDonald's should encourage its clientele to take up golf, I would urge you to look at the size of some of them and think how desperately they need the exercise. By subtly encouraging them to take up a healthy sport, you can claim to be doing your bit to combat obesity whilst continuing to flog essentially unhealthy burgers.

Called the 'McBunker', for reasons that will become apparent in a moment or two, my imaginative creation is something that you might care to promote at around the time of the Open Championship. Traditionally held in the middle of July, it is the undoubted highlight of the golfing calendar.

Okay, I sense you want to know the recipe. Well, between the two halves of your bog-standard bun, you first slap down a bed of boiled cabbage. This represents the grass on the fairways and greens. In a scooped-out bit in the middle, you plonk a large spoonful of scrambled eggs, which of course represents the sand in the bunker. As for the ball, a single egg of cod's roe would do. If anyone complains that cod's roe isn't very white, you should explain that golf balls aren't always white and the one in their McBunker is one of those that isn't.

Although I experimented with a number of various ingredients to represent the rake, including trying to bend soggy twiglets, in the end what I thought worked best was shoving a plastic T-shaped toothpick into the top of the bun that was both fun and, by holding the whole thing together, was functional as well.

And so there you have it – a comparatively healthy burger that promotes healthy exercise.

****

Dear Desert Island Discs,

What's happened to Roy Plumtree? I ask because I was listening to Desert Island Discs the other day for the first time in quite a while and there was some woman asking all the questions. I've nothing against women *per se*, you understand, but it just didn't sound right.

Anyway, my point is the programme is sounding rather tired, worse even than I do after 18 holes of golf. The problem, as I see it, is there are far too many what you might call celebrities and far too few ordinary people. Look back over the last 50 years or thereabouts and you could hardly claim your guest list is composed of a representative sample of humanity. Showbiz grotesquely outnumbers every other area of human endeavour while my extensive research has failed to reveal even one golfer. Mind you, I can't blame you for not inviting Sir Nick Faldo onto your show because he is irredeemably dull.

The problem with celebrities is they are rather inclined to bang on about their glitzy lifestyle leaving us Radio 4 listeners feeling like failures just because we never starred in a movie, had a number one hit, wrote a best-selling novel or won a Nobel Prize. The other thing about them is they choose music they think will impress listeners. We don't want dreary classical rubbish. Most people like music you can dance to or singalong with.

Assuming you're persuaded by the strength of my argument that you need more ordinary people to be marooned on your desert island where, you might wonder, will you find a decent cross-section of the nicer elements in our society? The answer might surprise you. Having spent a fair bit of my life in there, I can tell you that you need look no further than the spike bar at my local golf club. There are all sorts in there... scratch golfers, high handicappers, single figure players, the lot. There are even women!

To kick things off, you might care to invite me as I've a fund of riveting anecdotes and golf stories that I'm confident will amuse your listeners. That and some great music from the likes of Freddie and the Dreamers, the

Monkees, the Yardbirds and Billy Fury should make for a brilliant show. How about it, BBC?

****

Dear Talent Agency,

Although you may well not have heard of me, I am something of a celebrity at Dale Hill Hotel and Golf Club. It's impossible to be precise but I would estimate something like 63.8% of the members would recognise me. A weekday member for nearly 20 years, by conscientiously competing in most of the medals and virtually all the mid-week Stablefords, I have assiduously developed a high profile to the extent that I am generally regarded – and forgive me if I sound immodest - as one of the club's most popular characters.

My rise to fame, if I may call it that, climaxed around Christmas 2019 when I was asked if I would present the prizes at the Ladies Annual Dinner. Rumour has it that Colonel McDuffy had been booked but his gout flared up two days before the event, which would explain why I was given such short notice.

Despite that, my speech went down rather well. It's not easy to encapsulate a lifetime's adventures on the links in one short address and I thought I did well to keep it down to just three-quarters of an hour. It didn't help that a projector wasn't available and so I couldn't show slides of my golf trips to the Costa del Sol and North Wales. But I soldiered on and didn't allow the distinctly audible snoring emanating from the Lady Captain to distract me.

Anyway, having compiled such an extraordinary collection of riveting anecdotes, witty bon mots, sparkling jokes and fascinating observations on the nature of golf and life, it seems a great shame that, as things stand, it's highly unlikely that they will ever be aired again. Unless, that is, you can add me to your roster of outstanding speakers and secure me a string of engagements. Although golf is my greatest passion, I do know a great deal about, and can speak authoritatively on, a number of diverse topics including cheese labels, bee-keeping and breeding budgerigars.

Money has never been my god but I gather huge sums can be earned on the speaking circuit. Tony Blair, apparently, commands a six-figure fee. Well, three, or preferably four, figures will be enough for me, initially at least. Perhaps I could start with golf clubs and work my up to massive corporate occasions.

****

Dear Met Office,

Have you ever heard of Bryson DeChambeau? Don't worry if you haven't as I suspect he won't have heard of Michael Fish, Carol Kirkwood or Tomasz Schafernaker. Anyway, although he's rather slow when playing golf and, frankly, a bit of a 'nutter', he's nevertheless a very successful American golfer who's won quite a few important tournaments.

Rather like a lot of the boffins that I suspect work at the Met Office, he's something of a mad scientist. Anyway, he approaches golf in much the same way as you do the weather. For example, I don't suppose that you hang bits of seaweed outside your office or believe it's going to rain just because the cows are sitting down. Well, DeChambeau analyses all the data before taking a shot, which is one of the reasons he plays so slowly.

Although he's a bit creepy, you can't argue with his performances. At the time of writing, I think he's about number five in the world. Anyway, one of the vital variables he takes into account is air density and I'm wondering if there might be any commercial benefit to you in producing Air Density Forecasts. You needn't bother with the whole country just places like St Andrews, Sunningdale, The Belfry, Sandwich, Muirfield, etc.

I don't want to be paid for the idea, all I ask is that I be allowed to audition for the job of presenting the daily Air Density Forecasts on TV.

Yeah.. yeah... Im waiting for the Air Density App. to download, signals not the best out here!

Dear António Guterres,

What with wars, famine and disease, not to mention global pandemics, I appreciate that you've got your work cut out at the United Nations and I therefore hesitate to involve you in something which might at first glance appear to be quite trivial. However, because of the international nature of the problem I honestly believe that you are in an ideal position to sort it out.
Although I respect that different countries have different traditions and different ways of doing things, there are times when uniformity would be to everyone's benefit. Take plug sockets for example. If every country could agree to have the same number and shape pins, traveling would be much easier and you could take your hairdryer all over the world.
Since I'm an old man with very little hair, I'm less concerned about hair dryers than I am about golf. The specific problem that I've encountered on the golf courses of the world that you might be able to fix concerns the markers that indicate how far you are from the green.
Firstly, there are all sorts of different colours. Secondly, the markers are of varying distances from the green. Thirdly, they can be in either yards or metres. And, finally, sometimes they indicate the distance to the front of the green and sometimes to the centre.
As a result, the poor visiting golfer is utterly confused. (As indeed might you be if you're not a golfer and can't altogether appreciate the problem I'm trying to describe.) Although you might presume that this is something that the various governing bodies of golf should sort out I fear that, because of petty rivalries and jealousies, they won't. It therefore needs a respected global figure of great stature to intervene.

Initially, however, it might help if someone were to visit the principal golfing nations of the world. play on the main championship courses and report back to you. Now that I am more or less retired, I have the time and would be happy to take on this awesome task as an official UN Ambassador. Perhaps after you've raised the issue in the General Assembly and/or Security Council, you could let me know how much I'm going to earn and what sort of bar expenses would be considered acceptable.

****

Dear Rolex,

Although I know it sounds ridiculous, nothing in this world is more important to me than punctuality. Take this letter for example. The letterbox at the end of my road is emptied daily (except Sundays) at 4.45pm and so there I will be at 4.44pm this afternoon dropping it in. Because they care less about punctuality than I do, the Royal Mail often don't empty the box until after 5pm; I know because I can see it from my bedroom window.

Not only am I a remarkably punctual person, I am also a keen golfer. The two are not entirely unrelated as timing is a key component of the golf swing and turning up on the tee on time is absolutely vital, which brings me seamlessly onto the need to replace my present timepiece.

Unfortunately, the black silicone strap broke on my present watch at the top of my backswing hurling the important bit straight into the ball-washer thereby dislocating one of Mickey's arms. Sod's law dictated it was the right arm which, since you're in the business, you probably already know indicates the hour and so I now can tell it's, say, 20 minutes past something but 20 minutes past what?

Consequently, I can be an hour early or, much worse, an hour late, which is absolutely hopeless.
From reading your advertisements, I gather that you have struck deals with a number of top players. My suspicion is you probably give them a decent wedge (not lofted ☺) as well as one of your watches. Well, if you were to enrol me as a Rolex ambassador, you would only have to supply a watch as I wouldn't demand any money. Not only would I wear your watch with pride but I believe ordinary handicap golfers would also more easily identify with me than they would with a bunch of self-satisfied, super-rich, smug bastards who just so happen to be exceptionally good at golf.

****

Dear Senior Producer of the Archers,

I must confess that I don't listen to The Archers very often. However, on those infrequent occasions when I do, I quite enjoy it.
Having said that, I feel that the time has come to shift the social focus away from The Bull. Apart from anything else, I feel that it might, in some subliminal way, encourage drinking. Although I don't think it should be demolished to make way for an Ambridge bypass or be destroyed by a meteor, I do think that another regular venue should be found that has a healthier and more wholesome appeal.
Having given it a great deal of thought, I believe I have come up with the perfect solution. Since agriculture is almost certainly in terminal decline in this country, alternative uses must be found for farmland. And what better use could there possibly be than recreational?

So I suggest you convert a chunk of Home Farm (about 250 acres should be sufficient) into "Ambridge Golf and Country Club".

Golf is a great game and offers enormous opportunities for characters to interact. Then there are the competitions. Provided we can find a way to persuade the bulk of Ambridge inhabitants to quickly reach an acceptable standard of play, you could have sworn enemies meeting in the final of, say, the Walter Gabriel Memorial Trophy.

Mixed foursomes matches, traditionally rather fraught affairs, offer scope for all sorts of intrigue and naughtiness. If you decide to take-up my idea, by way of thanks, would you kindly audition me for the part of the club professional. Incidentally, if he's still alive, I think Jack Woolley would make an ideal club captain.

Section 6

Completely Daft

Dear Pfizer,

Before I go any further, would you kindly settle an argument that broke out in the spike bar of my golf club recently between myself and Harvey 'Three Putts' Harrison as to whether or not you pronounce the 'P' in Pfizer. My argument was that you **do** pronounce the 'P' otherwise why would it be there?

Before I go further still, may I congratulate you wholeheartedly on discovering a vaccine for that appalling Coronavirus thing that not only has killed dozens of people all over the world but caused the postponement of the US Masters, the cancellation of The Open and basically ruined my summer last year. I'm just hoping that I'm not among the unfortunate 10 per cent or thereabouts for whom your remedy apparently doesn't work.

Having dealt the pandemic a mortal blow, doubtless you are looking around wondering what to do next. After all, you can't afford to have all those white-coated boffins sitting around in your well-equipped laboratories twiddling their thumbs while waiting for the next nasty bug to escape from one of those disgusting Chinese markets where they sell all manner of diseased wild animals can you? In retrospect, I think my mother was absolutely right in refusing to ever eat in a Chinese restaurant. "You never know what's lurking beneath those huge piles of rice," she used to say.

Back to business. For some years now I have suffered from an affliction that blights the career of many a golfer for which, as yet, there is no known cure. Called the 'yips', its name suggests it might also have originated in China. Without going into too much detail, it's a sort of involuntary muscle spasm that renders putting an absolute nightmare. Golfers suffering from it would, I'm certain, pay vast sums to be cured.

If you would approach the problem with the same commitment, enthusiasm and determination you so admirably displayed when battling Coronavirus, I'm confident you could have a pill, vaccine or whatever available in all good pro shops before very long.
Finally, with regard to enrolling volunteers, I would happily put myself forward on condition you promise not to fob me off with some worthless placebo.

****

Dear Headmaster of Eton College,

I'm writing to enquire as to whether you would consider offering golf to your pupils as an alternative to the Wall Game. From the little I've seen of the latter, it seems decidedly rough and dangerous.
Not only is golf safe and civilised by comparison, it is also absolutely ideal for young toffs looking to make their way in the world of banking, stock broking, insider trading, money laundering and the like.
If you are prepared to consider it, I should like to offer my services as head golf coach. A 19 handicapper with an elegant shoulder turn but a rather strong grip, I honestly believe I could have won a couple of majors if only I had taken up the game earlier instead of wasting my time playing football. At the dodgy school I went to there was no choice. Now I'm keen to give others the chance that I never had.
Eton is fortunate in having plenty of playing fields, one of which could be used as a sort of driving range. And then I would hope there is a possibility that we could borrow the

nine-hole course I understand the infamous Prince Andrew has in a corner of Windsor Great Park.

No doubt you're quite chummy with the Royals and so a request from you will stand a much better chance of succeeding than one coming from me.

****

Dear European Tour,

In a world of finite resources where we all have a duty to conserve energy and reduce waste, how can professional golfers justify teeing up a brand new golf ball every couple of holes? Surely this is just profligate nonsense that flies in the face, not so much of bunkers, but of responsible behaviour. From my own considerable experience as a 19-handicapper, I can say with some authority that new balls behave no better and fly no further than averagely scuffed balls. So why do pros frequently discard a perfectly decent ball to tee up a new one? One obvious explanation is that they are given an endless supply of them for which they don't have to pay and so there's no incentive for them to be less wasteful.

Furthermore, the manufacture of golf balls clearly contributes to golf's carbon footprint and thus to climate change. Although my club (Dale Hill Hotel and Golf Club) is thankfully nearly 300 feet above sea level, the same is not true of the dozens of magnificent links courses stretched around our glorious coastline. Muirfield, Turnberry, Royal St George's, Rye, Royal Portrush, Trevose, Troon and dozens of others are extremely vulnerable to even a modest rise in sea level. Do we really want the Old Course at St Andrews to only be playable at low tide? Will we be happy that greenkeepers will not only rake the bunkers but drag seaweed off the greens as well? Of course not and so this is why the European Tour must introduce a rule that requires pros to only use one ball per round. If they lose it, they are out of the tournament.

Although this may sound harsh, in my opinion it will have the very beneficial effect of discouraging players from hitting the ball too far. For some time now the authorities have been worried about courses being overwhelmed by the 'bombers' but have been frightened to act for fear of being sued by the equipment manufacturers. Well, this could be the answer!

In recognition of helping to save both the planet and the game of golf, all I ask is that the new rule that requires players to only use one ball be called "Mortimer's Rule". In that way, although I've never won a major, my name will be immortalised so long as the game of golf is played.

Dear Guinness,

When people think of Ireland, which three things immediately spring to mind? Well, I believe they are Guinness, golf and dodgy priests doing unmentionable things to young children. Well, discarding the last one for reasons of good taste, let's focus on the other two - your magnificent beer and the greatest game on earth.

A creative thinker who makes a modest living by coming up with wholly original ideas to sell to large companies such as yours, I have what I believe is a genius proposal that I'm confident will boost consumption of Guinness wherever the game of golf is played.

Called the 'Guinness Golfball Giveaway', it's remarkably simple really and works like this. Whenever a customer orders a pint of Guinness, the barman or barwoman asks them, "Do you want to tee-off?" If the customer says "yes", the barman or barwoman proceeds to ask them a question about the Irish Open Golf Championship, such as, "Who won it in 1927?" If they answer, "George Duncan" and provided they buy another pint of Guinness, they go through to the next round.

In round two they have to answer a simple question on the rules of golf. For example, "If the player lifts his or her ball at rest or causes it to move, the ball must be replaced on its original spot (which if not known must be estimated) (see Rule 14.2), except in two specific circumstances, can you give me either of them?" The correct answer is either when the player lifts the ball under a Rule to take relief or to replace the ball on a different spot (see Rules 14.2d and 14.2e), or when the ball moves only after the player has begun the stroke or the backswing for a stroke and then goes on to make the stroke. It's entirely at the discretion of the barman or barwoman to decide whether the customer's answer is correct. If it is and provided they buy another pint, they can proceed to the third and final question on famous Irish golfers. Here the questions inevitably are a tad harder such as, how old was Christy O'Connor Snr when he died in 2016? The correct answer, of course, is 91. Everyone who gets three correct answers in a row wins a golf ball.

One of the great attractions of the 'Guinness Golfball Giveaway' is that it can easily be adapted to any country simply by tailoring the questions to that country. For example in Kazakhstan, question one would be about the Kazakhstan Open; question two would be about the rules of golf and question three would be about famous Kazakhstan golfers.

I'm happy to research and script all the questions for which I would ask a modest €10,000 per country.

****

Dear Sky Sports,

Until Sky appeared there was very little golf on TV and so I say 'well done' for bringing us so much great golf from around the world.

My purpose in writing is to make a suggestion that I think will improve your coverage considerably. Unlike football, where Sky has come up with a number of exciting innovations, the golf coverage has remained pretty much the same. One camera on the tee, another behind the green and occasionally one on the fairway with a sound man picking up the tedious discussion between player and caddie as to which way the wind is blowing.

Why not insert cameras into the heads of the putters of the main contenders? Then as the player lines up to stroke the ball, we at home will get a unique view of the putt. Admittedly, things might go a little awry as the player follows through after the putt but staying with it might provide some unusual shots of cloud formations and the like. You're not called Sky for nothing!

To anticipate a rather obvious concern that players won't welcome bulky cameras and attendant wires hanging off their putters, you know as well as I do that cameras these days are very small so that even the most sensitive players will hardly notice them.

If, as I expect, this proves enormously popular, you could extend the experiment to include other clubs such as drivers and the like. And another place they could be sited is in the flagsticks. A recent rule amendment allows players to leave the flag in when they putt. Perhaps you could lobby to make leaving the flag in compulsory and train the caddies to turn the stick so that the lens is facing whoever is putting. Caddies generally are accommodating chaps and would, I'm sure, be happy to cooperate, especially if you bung them a few beers after the round.

Ultimately, of course, a camera inside the ball offers the unbelievably exciting prospect of a totally fresh perspective on the game. But that, like the players' unbelievable drives, might be way off in the distance.

****

Dear FootJoy,

The traffic is horrific, and it looks like you're going to be late on the first tee and incur a two-shot penalty or, worse still, be disqualified. You pull up in the car park but you've not yet changed your shoes. Don't panic because you're wearing a pair of Kwikswitcher shoes. Just leap out of the car and clip a pair of spiked soles onto them – soft or hard spikes depending on the conditions. And then crunch an imperious drive down the first.

On the tricky par three, you hit your tee-shot a bit fat and just fail to carry the stream that guards the green. Your ball is lying in shallow water and is distinctly playable but you don't want to play the rest of the round with wet feet. Nor do you want to take a penalty drop. Fortunately, you've remembered the 'growtall' attachment is in your bag and so you simply unclip your spiked soles and snap on the six-inch platform soles. After you've splashed out, you stick your spikes back on and hole the putt for par. (Incidentally, I tried installing the platforms inside the shoes so that they would automatically inflate when they made contact with water, in much the same way as do lifeboats in aircraft, but I experienced too many mishaps when simply striding down slightly soggy fairways).

Back to our story. You win the match and, as you walk off the 18th green, your dejected opponent shakes your hand and then disappears into the locker-room to change his shoes whereas all you have to do is unclip your spikes and, hey presto, you're now back into town shoes and ready for that celebratory pint.

You will be aware of how expensive shoes are these days, especially decent golf shoes. What shall we say, £100? So three pairs will cost £300. Instead, a pair of Kwikswitchers will only set you back a modest £125, thus saving you £175! And you can save a whole lot more when you buy any of the numerous accessories including snap-on ice-blades, crampons, football boots, ballet shoes and roller-blades.

Since my knowledge of the boot and shoe industry is somewhat limited, I'm wondering if you would like to buy my patented design and take over the entire project. Does £250,000 all-in sound reasonable?

Dear Andy Murray,

First of all, belated congratulations on winning so many tennis matches during your extremely illustrious career. Mrs Merriweather is a huge fan of yours and, frankly, has been inconsolable since your decision to more or less retire. But as I, too, have a dodgy hip, I can probably empathise with your plight more than she can. Incidentally, may I politely enquire as how you were able to have your recent operation organised so quickly when I've been waiting ages for mine? Perhaps the NHS queue north of the border is shorter than it is in Sussex. Well, I suppose it's only fair there are compensations for living in such a bleak place with such awful weather surrounded by the likes of that dreadful Alex Salmond and having to listen to dreary bagpipes.
Anyway, while you're considering what you're going to do in the future, may I make a suggestion? Although you will doubtless be tempted to take up commentating or coaching tennis, I would urge you to continue competing, but at golf not tennis. Golf is so much better than tennis; it's much friendlier, apart from the occasional 'fore!' no one yells and it's a lot less tiring.
I read somewhere that, although Jamie was better, you were a half-decent single-figure player in your youth until you foolishly switched to tennis. With a few lessons, I'm sure you would soon be playing well enough to compete on the European Tour. Remember, golfers traditionally don't peak until their mid-30s and so time is on your side. To the best of my knowledge, no one has ever won a tennis grand slam AND a golf major. By becoming the first, you would secure your place in the pantheon of great British sportsmen and, because I know you're a bit funny about it, sportswomen.
As you are already fairly well-known, I'm absolutely certain that, if you did become a pro golfer, you would

receive dozens of sponsors' invites to play in the very best, most lucrative tournaments. You would only need to make a few cuts and secure the odd top-ten finish to earn enough to retain your card and stay on the tour.

To help keep the cost down, I'd be willing to carry your bag for free – for the first couple of years at least. "Mortimer and Murray", has a ring to it, don't you think?

Come on, Andy – let's do it!

****

Dear Michael O'Leary,

"Mr O'Leary is a commercial genius," I told my wife recently when we were flying with Ryanair from Shannon to Gatwick after a lovely golfing holiday in County Clare. To be precise, because we were sitting 15 rows apart as a result of your inspired policy of separating travelling companions unless they're prepared to stump up the extra, I said it to her as we were walking into the south terminal at Gatwick.

Of all your innovations, I think extorting a penal charge from suckers who, for whatever reason, don't have a boarding pass is perhaps your single greatest contribution to modern travel. Anyway, I have a suggestion which, if implemented, should provide a fitting boost to what appears to be your sagging bottom line.

Not that it matters to you one grimy Euro how rich or poor are the customers you fleece but there is, perhaps, a tad more satisfaction in ripping off the rich. Anyway, golfers generally are fairly well off and so could be regarded as legitimate targets. Although you already charge a fair bit for carrying clubs in the hold, there is undoubted scope for squeezing a bit more from the unwary hackers. Since no golfer has a clue as to what the circumference of his bag is, you could apply a maximum limit of, say, 25 inches which, although sounding generous, would catch out all but the smallest bags. Trust me, very few would slip through the net. Alternatively, you could stipulate a maximum of 13 clubs which, since nearly every golfer has a full-set of 14, should generate substantial extra revenue. Or why not do both and enjoy a double bonanza? Doubtless you have a 'Fleecing Unit' which could assess my suggestions and I hardly need advise you, or them, of the need to slip something in very small type somewhere near the bottom of the terms and conditions. Renowned for respecting the rules, golfers should take the penalty on the chin.

****

Dear DJ Spoony,

As a black man yourself, you will be aware of the awful prejudice that exists in many sectors of our society. And, as a golfer, you know that, to its enormous shame, the game which we both love has hardly blazed the progressive trail in recognising the fundamental equality of human beings. Sadly, we still can't claim that all golfers will be welcome everywhere regardless of race, creed, colour, religion, sex and handicap. A black woman playing off, say, six should be just as welcome at any golf club as a white, middle-aged man with a dodgy grip and a handicap in the 20s. However, golf remains a bastion of reactionary forces who seem determined to resist much-needed change.

As an occasional weekend player, I'm frequently shocked both by the appalling prejudices manifested by my playing partners and, even more insulting, the casual assumption they make that I must share their ugly opinions. To my considerable shame, rather than disabuse them, I simply say nothing and hope that they might cotton on to the fact that I don't agree with them.

What I've been searching for is a discreet but effective way of indicating to those with whom I play golf that I'm not bigoted and I'd rather they kept their unfunny racist jokes to themselves. The solution came to me on the short 15th at Dale Hill Hotel and Golf Club ... a black ball. Because it symbolises rejection, a black ball would, in my opinion, be a particularly appropriate method of conveying the message, "Shut up, bigot!"

What I'm suggesting, therefore, is that an approach be made to one of the major golf ball manufacturers urging them to produce a ball and make a modest donation to Black Lives Matter for every one sold. After fairly extensive field tests with a few that I painted myself, I found them perfectly satisfactory in every respect other than they are fiendishly difficult to follow in flight and then to find. Still, I'm confident "we will overcome" this slight obstacle.

Your support in this venture would be greatly appreciated.

Dear Head of Research and Development at Blue Line Office Furniture,

You will be aware, I'm sure, of the strong liking our captains of industry and business leaders have for the game of golf. Even the very briefest of glances through "Who's Who" and the hobbies of the rich and famous reveals an astonishing fondness for it.

Furthermore, I believe that this fact can be commercially exploited by a combination of my considerable knowledge of the game and your well-deserved reputation in the wacky world of office furniture.

I therefore propose that we jointly examine the feasibility of reproducing some of the most famous greens in the world in the offices of some of the most powerful men and women on the planet.

If you've ever watched golf on television, you will have seen the computer-generated graphics that are often used to illustrate the slope on a green. All the information that we need, therefore, is already available and I don't suppose it would be much of a problem to persuade the relevant TV companies to release it to us.

All we would need to do is convert this information into three dimensional carpets with some form of foam supporting the raised areas. The foam would need to be fairly resilient in order to create an authentic turf-like feel and care would need to be taken to ensure that the texture of the surface material, the carpet if you like, possesses similar qualities to a close-cut lawn so that putting on it would be just like putting on the green itself. We could even check the speed of the carpets with the same device used by tournament officials, a stimpmeter.

The only problem I can foresee is making adjustments to the rest of the office furniture to allow for the slope. For example, three of the legs on the desk might need to be shortened to ensure that the top was horizontal. Because this furniture might get moved around, rather than simply saw off legs at the bottom, it would perhaps be desirable to make the legs adjustable.

And I would suggest the hole itself be movable to even out the wear and tear and to provide the occupant with a variety of challenging putts. I suggest we start with a range of 18th greens taken from such great courses as St Andrews, Wentworth, Carnoustie, Pebble Beach and Augusta. These could be split into ranges. How about the British Open, Ryder Cup and US Open with six in each?

Clearly with offices being predominantly rectangular and of different sizes, we would simply take a rectangular chunk out of each green. Bunkers in the form of sunken sofas could be an optional extra.

****

THE END

Printed in Great Britain
by Amazon